HOW TO BUY
GOVERNMENT SURPLUS

BY

JOHN ANDERSON

ISBN 0-934748-24-1

Manufactured in the United States of America

PUBLISHER'S NOTE

We have done our best to carefully research and compile this directory only from sources believed to be authentic and reliable; however, we cannot guarantee total accuracy or completeness.

If you would be kind enough to bring to our attention any errors you may find, we will include your corrections in our next edition. We will also send you a complimentary copy of one of our other reports as a token of our appreciation.

Please note we are publishers and are not affiliated in any way with the U.S. Government or any agency mentioned in this Directory. Our sole purpose is to provide you with a lot of useful information.

Good luck in your surplus buying!

THE PUBLISHERS

Acknowledgement

The material in this Directory is drawn in part from government publications. Their contribution is gratefully acknowledged.

CONTENTS

APPENDICES

LIST OF FIGURES

1.0   FOREWORD

HOW WOULD YOU LIKE TO BUY A PICKUP WITH AN
INVENTORY VALUE OF $6,135.00 for **only $257**?

.... OR A SEDAN
INVENTORY VALUE $6,355.00 for **only $70**?

Sound unbelieveable?   Well, it's a <u>fact</u>!   These and other amazing bargains were recently sold at a Government Surplus Sale.   Turn to Figures 2 and 3, pages 18 and 19, to see for yourself.

You've already taken the first important step toward getting these great bargins for yourself -- you bought this directory.   And incidentally, there is no other directory we've ever seen which is as detailed and understandable as the one you're now reading.

BEFORE YOU EVEN SPEND TIME READING THE DETAILS, YOU SHOULD GET YOUR BARGAIN HUNTING STARTED RIGHT NOW BY GETTING YOUR NAME ON THE MAILING LISTS SO YOU CAN START RECEIVING INFORMATION ABOUT THE SALES AS SOON AS POSSIBLE.   THESE ARE <u>FREE</u>!

To make this easy for you, we have enclosed two postcards for you; just fill them out and mail them (<u>today!</u>) -- then read on.

<u>FIRST:</u>
To receive the Surplus Property Bidder's Application form from DoD, send in card #1 (simply cut out the card from the enclosed sheet).

<u>SECOND:</u>
To receive the GSA Surplus Personal Property Mailing List Application, send in card #2 (cut out the card from the enclosed sheet).

<u>THIRD:</u>
Start reading all about it!

2.0   INTRODUCTION

What, **exactly,** is government surplus?   As mentioned in Section 1.0, the items involved include vehicles of all kinds and real estate, but it goes far beyond these items.   Anything and everything you can imagine from office equipment and supplies to houses and housewares to engines and tires -- the list could go on forever.

WHY should the government want to sell these good items to you?   Or, are the items good?   Is the government trying to unload its junk and make a profit at the same time?

It should come as no surprise to you that government agencies tend to over-buy on items they need (particularly the military agencies) so they won't run out at a critical point and be unable to do their jobs.   Oftentimes items which have been in storage (and which have never even been used) become outdated for an agency, or a project will end, before they use the items.   The agency must then do some "housekeeping" to get rid of the unused items, and they become government surplus.

The situation with vehicles varies widely.   Yes, it's true that many of the vehicles are extremely well-used, but depending upon what use the cars (trucks, etc.) were purchased for in the first place, many may have few miles on them and they may be in extremely good condition.   In the case of very used (poor condition) vehicles, the government sells these for parts ... parts which are inexpensive to the purchaser, but which helps the government to recoup some of the initial cost paid for the vehicle.   This is a great "win-win" situation for the taxpayer who buys surplus: you get parts very cheaply and it takes less taxes to help buy new equipment.   This applies not only to car parts, but to many other surplus items as well.

The Department of Defense (DoD) and the General Services Administration (GSA) are two of the principal government agencies engaged in selling surplus property.   In addition to selling surplus property, several other government agencies also sell personal property which was seized from private citizens -- for example, IRS tax seizures, U.S. Customs seizures, Drug Enforcement Administration seizures, and so on.

Other than the Department of Defense and the General Services Administration, the most important sources of surplus and seized property are:

The U.S. Postal Service
The U.S. Customs Service
The Internal Revenue Service (IRS)
The U.S. Small Business Administration (SBA)

In-depth information on each of these agencies is provided in the pages which follow, as well as other valuable information which you should find helpful.

3.0 BUYING FROM THE DEPARTMENT OF DEFENSE

The DoD sells surplus from the many military installations throughout the United States. Anything that can be used on a military base can be sold through the DoD's surplus sales. Therefore, this section will cover a great deal of information and is very comprehensive; it may be helpful for you to write notes in the margins as you go in order to pick out the sections which are of the most interest to you.

The first step is to start receiving your auction catalogs from DoD. If you have filled out and mailed in the postcard provided for you, your auction catalogs should begin arriving within a few weeks.

If you have not mailed in your postcard yet, you should do so now, before reading further. You'll be anxious to get to your first auction, so avoid delay by filling your postcard out right away.

3.1 THE "SPH" -- SALES PERFORMANCE HISTORY REPORTS

As a beginner at surplus buying, you may be interested in finding out how much other people have paid in the past for certain items. The SPH (or Sales Performance History) report is an excellent tool which shows what property was sold, when and where it was sold and the price it was sold for. Let me say that this is about the only item of information I've found which isn't free. There is a charge which depends upon the amount of computer time taken to print the computer output you request. Therefore, the more information you request, the more you will be charged. KEEP IN MIND THAT YOU **DO NOT** HAVE TO BUY ONE OF THESE REPORTS IN ORDER TO BID ON SURPLUS PROPERTY. SPH reports are merely a source of information to help you decide how much to bid.

In order for you to see how valuable the SPH report can be, let's suppose you want to buy a car. FIGURE 1 on page 11 shows a page of the "USABLE SURPLUS PROPERTY PERFORMANCE HISTORY REPORT" (SPH) for cars. Take a close look at it, and I'll explain exactly what it means. Don't worry if you don't understand it all at first; there's a lot of information to look at, and it will become clearer to you as you progress through this directory. Beginning at the left-hand column, here are the official definitions along with some comments:

USABLE SURPLUS PROPERTY PERFORMANCE HISTORY REPORT

OPTIONS: FSG =   CL-OF-SUR = 2310A   DRMR =   PHY LOC =   M/S =   C/C =   REPORTING PERIOD: 86043 THRU 87043   PAGE 3

FIGURE 1
USABLE SURPLUS PROPERTY
PERFORMANCE HISTORY REPORT
(SEDANS)

NSN = 2310000000000A for all rows.

CLASS OF SURP	ITEM NAME	U/I	QTY SOLD	FED C/C	INVENTORY VALUE	UNIT BID PRICE	M/S	SALES PROCEEDS	C/C	% RET	ITEM NO.	IFB NO.	M/S	BOD	D/A	PHY LOC	NBR	BDR ID	ZIP CODE
SEDAN	SEDAN	EA	1.00	H9	3011	178.000000	.000000	178		5.91	080	276009	B	85317	1	AA	001	3000306843	12962
SEDAN	SEDAN	EA	1.00	HX	5	.000000	.000000	0		.00	172	276114	F	86008	2	AFG	000		
SEDAN	SEDAN	EA	1.00	FX	2500	55.000000	.000000	55		2.20	145	276172	F	86044	1	JO	001		02904
SEDAN	SEDAN	EA	1.00	HX	75	160.000000	.000000	160		213.33	155	276164	F	86051	1	FSC	001		63050
SEDAN	SEDAN	EA	1.00	F8	4076	600.000000	.000000	600		14.72	150	276164	F	86051	1	FSC	001		60515
SEDAN	SEDAN	EA	1.00	F8	4031	25.000000	.000000	25		.62	147	276164	F	86042	1	FSC	001		62060
SEDAN	SEDAN	EA	1.00	F9	3244	190.000000	.000000	190		5.86	162	276134	F	86037	1	JL	001		06484
SEDAN	SEDAN	EA	1.00	HX	25	20.000000	.000000	20		80.00	180	276213	F	86078	1	FRM	001		20621
SEDAN	SEDAN	EA	1.00	H8	7284	150.000000	.000000	150		2.06	201	275378	F	85240	1	DCS	001		43055
SEDAN	SEDAN	EA	1.00	HX	4000	25.000000	.000000	25		.63	199	275307	F	85176	1	NCH	001		22503
SEDAN	SEDAN	EA	1.00	HX	75	80.000000	.000000	80		106.67	175	276032	F	85311	1	FG	001		13440
SEDAN	SEDAN	EA	1.00	HX	3205	95.000000	.000000	95		2.96	172	276032	F	85311	1	FRM	001		20659
SEDAN	SEDAN	EA	1.00	HX	3825	80.000000	.000000	80		2.09	232	276040	F	85317	1	FRM	001		20662
SEDAN	SEDAN	EA	1.00	HX	25	350.000000	.000000	350		******	229	276040	F	85317	2	A4	001		01545
SEDAN	SEDAN	EA	1.00	HX	25	25.000000	.000000	25		100.00	226	276040	F	85317	1	A4	001		01420
SEDAN	SEDAN	EA	1.00	HX	35	.000000	.000000	0		.00	215	276040	F	85317	2	A4	000		
SEDAN	SEDAN	EA	1.00	HX	100	.000000	.000000	0		.00	212	276040	F	85317	2	A4	000		
SEDAN	SEDAN	EA	1.00	HX	5205	350.000000	.000000	350		6.72	209	276040	F	85317	1	A4	001		01368
SEDAN	SEDAN	EA	1.00	HX	500	60.000000	.000000	60		12.00	325	276033	F	85339	1	FRM	001		22042
SEDAN	SEDAN	EA	1.00	HX	25	5.000000	.000000	5		20.00	322	276033	F	85339	1	FRM	001		22503
SEDAN	SEDAN	EA	1.00	HX	500	150.000000	.000000	150		30.00	319	276033	F	85339	1	DCS	001		20662
SEDAN	SEDAN	EA	1.00	H8	2752	150.000000	.000000	150		5.45	168	276213	F	86078	1	DCS	001		45645
SEDAN	SEDAN	EA	1.00	H9	7284	125.000000	.000000	125		1.72	165	276213	F	86078	1	ARL	001		43207
SEDAN	SEDAN	EA	1.00	HX	101	60.000000	.000000	60		59.41	256	276209	F	86078	1	ARL	001		66517
SEDAN	SEDAN	EA	1.00	HX	101	33.000000	.000000	33		32.67	253	276209	F	86064	1	ARL	001		66517
SEDAN	SEDAN	EA	1.00	HX	101	13.000000	.000000	13		12.87	212	276201	F	86064	1	FRM	001		64501
SEDAN	SEDAN	EA	1.00	HX	50	5.000000	.000000	5		10.00	236	276194	F	86093	1	FRM	001		22503
SEDAN	SEDAN	EA	1.00	HX	2928	90.000000	.000000	90		3.07	161	276179	F	86070	1	A4	001		01468
SEDAN	SEDAN	EA	1.00	HX	50	30.000000	.000000	30		60.00	075	276179	F	86070	1	A4	001		01420
SEDAN	SEDAN	EA	1.00	HX	25	40.000000	.000000	40		160.00	072	276179	F	86070	1	A4	001		01468
SEDAN	SEDAN	EA	1.00	HX	25	25.000000	.000000	25		100.00	069	276179	F	86070	1	A4	001		01432
SEDAN	SEDAN	EA	1.00	HX	101	310.000000	.000000	310		306.93	227	275317	F	85177	1	ARL	001		66517
SEDAN	SEDAN	EA	1.00	HX	101	10.000000	.000000	10		9.90	224	275317	F	85177	1	ARL	001		66508
SEDAN	SEDAN	EA	1.00	HX	50	325.000000	.000000	325		650.00	241	275317	F	85177	1	ARL	001		66517
SEDAN	SEDAN	EA	1.00	HX	50	.000000	.000000	0		.00	180	276203	F	86203	2	NSG	000		60085
SEDAN	SEDAN	EA	1.00	HX	50	50.000000	.000000	50		.69	167	276354	F	86204	1	NSG	000		
SEDAN	SEDAN	EA	1.00	HX	7284	50.000000	.000000	50		.69	193	276419	F	86204	1	ASG	001		61530
SEDAN	SEDAN	EA	1.00	F7	3500	1700.000000	.000000	1700		48.57	232	276398	F	86210	1	ANJ	001		07305
SEDAN	SEDAN	EA	1.00	HX	5377	325.000000	.000000	325		6.04	229	276398	F	86210	1	ANJ	001		10467
SEDAN	SEDAN	EA	1.00	FX	3232	5.000000	.000000	5		.00	225	276398	F	86210	2	ANJ	001		07060
SEDAN	SEDAN	EA	1.00	F7	4000	1850.000000	.000000	1850		46.25	221	276398	F	86210	1	ANJ	001		07306

CLASS OF SURPLUS - NSN

This is the Government's stock number assigned to each type of surplus. The first 4 digits are the Class of Surplus, suffix letter indicated subgroup, if any, within the Class. See Appendix 1: "Index to Classes of Surplus Personal Property," page 78 of this manual, for a comprehensive list of stock numbers (over 460) and the types of surplus they apply to.

ITEM NAME

The common name of the property sold.

U/I

Unit of Issue (e.g., EA = each; LT = lot; LB = pound).

QTY SOLD

Quantity sold.

FED C/C

Federal Condition Code (detailed in Section 3.1.1 below).

INVENTORY VALUE

The dollar value at which material is carried on inventory records for government accounting purposes. It is established on the basis of standard prices (or actual or estimated acquisition cost of items when standard prices are not used). This is applicable to all property regardless of condition; it does not, therefore, necessarily reflect a true value based on Condition Code.

UNIT BID PRICE

The bid received for each unit sold in that particular item number.

SALE PROCEEDS

Total revenue received for sale of item(s).

% RET.

Percent return (Unit bid price divided by Inventory Value).

ITEM NO.

This is the number assigned to the item in the IFB (sales catalog).

IFB NO.

Number of the IFB (sales catalog) in which the item was listed for sale.

M/S

Method of Sale (A = Auction; B = Sealed Bid (one time); T = Sealed Bid (term); N = Negotiated (one time); P = Negotiated (term); S = Spot Bid; L = Local Spot Bid; F = Local Auction).

BOD

Bid Opening Date. The first two digits represent the current year, and the last 3 digits are the day of the year sequentially numbered (out of 365 days). For example, 87081 means the year 1987 and the 81st day of the year, or March 22, 1987.

D/A

Disposition Action Code. This tells what actually happened to each item:

1 = Sold (property paid for and removed)
2 = No bid -- returned to holding activity
3 = No bid -- being held for future sale
4 = Bid rejected -- control returned to holding activity; recommend scrap
5 = Bid rejected -- held for future sales
6 = (No 6?)
7 = Item withdrawn for other than utilization (i.e., a wrong description)
8 = Sale cancelled (i.e., 70% of the sale withdrawn for utilization, the 30% will be coded 8)
9 = Alternate bid item, or items making up an alternate bid and not awarded
A = Withdrawn -- utilization -- requested by holding activity
B = Withdrawn -- utilization -- requested by DPDS
C = Withdrawn -- utilization -- requested by holding activity after cataloging

D = Withdrawn -- utilization -- requested by DPDS after cataloging

E = Withdrawn -- utilization -- after award

Z = Default

PHY LOC
Physical location of the item for sale.

NBR
Number of bids received for that particular item.

BDR ID
Identification number of successful bidder, as assigned by Bidder's Control Office.

ZIP CODE
Zip Code of successful bidder.

Directly above the columns just described, you'll notice a line that begins with the word **OPTIONS.** This simply indicates the type of data listed on the page. A blank space after "=" sign indicates one or more different varieties for that data element. The **REPORTING PERIOD** is the time period covered by the report. The first 2 digits are the year, and the last 3 digits are the day of the year sequentially numbered.

3.1.1   FEDERAL CONDITION CODES

The following codes were referred to above under "FED C/C" -- these are the codes which explain what condition each item is in:

A -- Serviceable (Issuable without Qualification)
New, used, repaired or reconditioned material which is serviceable and issuable to all customers without limitation or restriction. Includes material with more than 6 months of shelf-life remaining.

B -- Serviceable (Issuable with Qualification)
New, used, repaired and reconditioned material which is serviceable and issuable for its intended purpose but which is restricted from issue to specific units, activities or geographical areas by reason of its limited usefulness or short service-life expectancy. Includes material with 3 through 6 months shelf-life expectancy.

C — Serviceable (Priority Issue)

Items which are serviceable and issuable to selected customers, but which must be issued before Condition A and B material to avoid loss as a usable asset. Includes material with less than 3 months shelf-life remaining.

D — Serviceable (Test/Modification)

Serviceable material which requires test, alteration, modification, conversion or disassembly. (This does not include items which must be inspected or tested immediately prior to issue).

E — Unserviceable (Limited Restoration)

Material which involves only limited expense or effort to restore to serviceable condition and which is accomplished in the storage activity where the stock is located.

F — Unserviceable (Reparable)

Economically reparable material which requires repair, overhaul, or reconditioning. Includes reparable items which are radioactively contaminated.

G — Unserviceable (Incomplete)

Material requiring additional parts or components to complete the end item prior to issue.

H — Unserviceable (Condemned)

Material which has been determined to be unserviceable and does not meet repair criteria (includes condemned items which are radioactively contaminated).

P — Unserviceable (Reclamation)

Material determined to be unserviceable, uneconomically reparable as a result of physical inspection, tear down or engineering decision. Item contains serviceable components or assemblies to be reclaimed.

S — Unserviceable (Scrap)

Material that has no value except for its basic material content. No stock will be recorded as on hand in condition Code S. This code is used only on transactions involving shipments to DPDOs. Material will not be transferred to Condtiion S Code prior to turn in to PDOs if material is recorded in Condition A through H at the time material is determined excess. Material identified by NSN will not be identified by this condition code.

1 — Unused — Good

Unused property that is usable without repairs and identical or interchangeable with new items from normal supply sources.

2 — Unused — Fair

Unused property that is usable without repairs, but is deteriorated or damaged to the extent that utility is somewhat impaired.

3 — Unused — Poor

Unused property that is usable without repairs, but is considerably deteriorated or damaged. Enough utility remains to classify the property better than salvage.

4 — Used — Good

Used property that is usable without repairs and most of its useful life remains.

5 — Used — Fair

Used property that is usable without repairs, but is somewhat worn or deteriorated and may soon require repairs.

6 — Used — Poor

Used property that may be used without repairs, but is considerably worn or deteriorated to the degree that remaining utility is limited or major repairs will soon be required.

7 — Repairs Required — Good

Required repairs are minor and should not exceed 15% of original acquisition cost.

8 — Repairs Required — Fair

Required repairs are considerable and are estimated to range from 16% to 40% of original acquisition cost.

9 — Repairs Required — Poor

Required repairs are major because the property is badly damaged, worn, or deteriorated, and are estimated to range from 41% to 65% of original acquisition cost.

X - Salvage

Property has some value in excess of its basic material content, but repair or rehabilitation to use for the originally intended purpose is clearly impractical. Repair for any use would exceed 65% of the original acquisition cost. DPDS NOTE: Code X applies only to items identified with a NSN or LSN.

S — Scrap

Material that has no value except for its basic material content.

 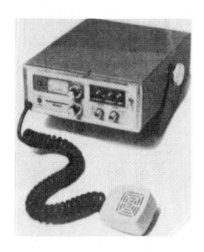 

In further examining the SPH, take a look at FIGURES 2 and 3 on the following pages; they show similar history reports for station wagons, pickup trucks, cargo trucks and ambulances. These particular reports cover the sales period from February 12, 1986 through February 12, 1987 and include sales data for 7,537 vehicles. The average price for a car was $155.89, and the average price for a truck was $363.56. Even if you purchase a vehicle that needs repairs, for these low prices, you'll still get a bargain. As you can see, there really is a lot of opportunity for you to find these items or the thousand-and-one other items you want <u>at very low prices!</u>

In any event, there is an enormous amount of information available to you in these SPH reports if you can use it; it may well be that you can specify printouts of only very specific items of equipment and/or locations

USABLE SURPLUS PROPERTY PERFORMANCE HISTORY REPORT

OPTIONS: FSG =   CL-OF-SUR = 2320D   DRMR =   PHY LOC =   M/S =   C/C =   REPORTING PERIOD: 86043 THRU 87043   PAGE 20

NSN SUR/CM-ID CLASS OF SURP	ITEM NAME	U/I	QTY SOLD	FED C/C	INVENTORY VALUE	UNIT BID PRICE	SALES PROCEEDS	% RET	ITEM NO.	IFB NO.	M/S	BOD	D/A	PHY LOC	PHY NBR	BDR ID	ZIP CODE
23200000000000D	TRUCK PCIKUP	EA	1.00	H9	1000	275.000000	275	27.50	247	416266	F	86080	1	NBM	001		92311
23200000000000D	TRUCK PCKUP	EA	1.00	HX	2080	33.000000	33	1.59	158	315124	L	84340	1	NL	001		33043
23200000000000D	TRUCK PHONE	EA	1.00	HX	3050	175.000000	175	5.74	183	276300	F	86156	1	NSG	001		60085
23200000000000D	TRUCK PICK U	EA	1.00	HX	500	1581.000000	1581	316.20	249	316252	F	86063	1	NDO	001		39503
23200000000000D	TRUCK PICK U	EA	1.00	F9	2003	450.000000	450	22.47	217	416334	F	86113	1	ASC	001		95204
23200000000000D	TRUCK PICK U	EA	1.00	F9	3215	50.000000	50	1.56	285	416315	F	86107	1	NSY	001		95452
23200000000000D	TRUCK PICK U	EA	1.00	HX	5000	50.000000	50	1.00	180	416204	F	86042	1	FED	001		93516
23200000000000D	TRUCK PICK-U	EA	1.00	F9	5454	425.000000	425	7.79	197	276110	F	86007	1	DGS	001		23234
23200000000000D	TRUCK PICK-U	EA	1.00	HX	50	475.000000	475	950.00	177	276300	F	86156	1	NSG	001		53182
23200000000000D	TRUCK PICK-U	EA	1.00	HX	3615	433.000000	433	11.98	219	276197	F	86084	1	NSG	001		53066
23200000000000D	TRUCK PICK-U	EA	1.00	FX	6135	252.000000	252	4.11	164	276069	L	85325	1	FG	001		13054
23200000000000D	TRUCK PICK-U	EA	1.00	FX	2700	326.000000	326	12.07	236	276261	L	86119	1	NNS	001		15940
23200000000000D	TRUCK PICK-U	EA	1.00	FX	6135	251.000000	251	9.30	238	276261	L	86119	1	NNS	001		16823
23200000000000D	TRUCK PICK-U	EA	1.00	F9	6135	377.000000	377	6.15	172	276069	L	85325	1	FG	001		13309
23200000000000D	TRUCK PICK-U	EA	1.00	F9	4169	257.000000	257	4.19	056	276117	F	86009	1	FG	001		13440
23200000000000D	TRUCK PICK-U	EA	1.00	HX	1390	250.000000	250	6.00	249	316610	F	86224	1	FK	001		39532
23200000000000D	TRUCK PICK-U	EA	1.00	FX	2313	276.000000	276	19.86	250	316262	L	86071	1	FCR	001		76133
23200000000000D	TRUCK PICK-U	EA	1.00	HX	3430	265.000000	265	11.46	245	316610	F	86224	1	FK	001		39574
23200000000000D	TRUCK PICKUP	EA	1.00	HX	600	240.000000	240	7.00	199	276053	F	85344	1	NCE	001		23322
23200000000000D	TRUCK PICKUP	EA	1.00	HX	3313	200.000000	200	33.33	167	276039	F	85316	1	NSV	001		23321
23200000000000D	TRUCK PICKUP	EA	1.00	HX	5119	90.000000	90	2.72	185	276272	F	86126	1	NCE	001		23707
23200000000000D	TRUCK PICKUP	EA	1.00	FX	4153	225.000000	225	4.40	075	276274	F	86191	1	FRM	001		21157
23200000000000D	TRUCK PICKUP	EA	1.00	HX	2926	360.000000	360	8.67	245	276294	F	86176	1	NMQ	001		22314
23200000000000D	TRUCK PICKUP	EA	1.00	FX	1521	30.000000	30	1.03	058	276309	F	86156	1	JO	001		02886
23200000000000D	TRUCK PICKUP	EA	1.00	HX	3313	35.000000	35	2.30	055	276309	F	86156	1	JO	001		02886
23200000000000D	TRUCK PICKUP	EA	1.00	HX	3313	120.000000	120	3.62	217	276329	F	86161	1	NCE	001		23509
23200000000000D	TRUCK PICKUP	EA	1.00	HX	4932	200.000000	200	4.06	213	276329	F	86161	1	NCE	001		23503
23200000000000D	TRUCK PICKUP	EA	1.00	FX	516	350.000000	350	67.83	187	276321	F	86169	1	FL	001		12303
23200000000000D	TRUCK PICKUP	EA	1.00	FX	4500	250.000000	250	5.56	064	276355	F	86196	1	NCE	001		23509
23200000000000D	TRUCK PICKUP	EA	1.00	HX	2948	175.000000	175	5.94	087	276355	F	86196	1	NCE	001		23509
23200000000000D	TRUCK PICKUP	EA	1.00	HX	4137	125.000000	125	3.02	084	276355	F	86196	1	NCE	001		23503
23200000000000D	TRUCK PICKUP	EA	1.00	FX	2948	150.000000	150	5.09	081	276355	F	86196	1	NCE	001		23322
23200000000000D	TRUCK PICKUP	EA	1.00	FX	3200	75.000000	75	2.34	068	276355	F	86196	1	NSV	001		27944
23200000000000D	TRUCK PICKUP	EA	1.00	FX	600	125.000000	125	20.83	164	276039	F	85316	1	NSV	001		23503
23200000000000D	TRUCK PICKUP	EA	1.00	HX	5882	150.000000	150	2.55	062	276179	F	86070	1	A4	001		23503
23200000000000D	TRUCK PICKUP	EA	1.00	HX	4940	40.000000	40	.81	159	276172	F	86044	1	JO	001		03901
23200000000000D	TRUCK PICKUP	EA	1.00	FX	2300	350.000000	350	15.22	175	276172	F	86044	1	JO	001		02827
23200000000000D	TRUCK PICKUP	EA	1.00	HX	500	10.000000	10	2.00	183	276214	F	86157	1	NCH	001		02920
23200000000000D	TRUCK PICKUP	EA	1.00	F9	1200	650.000000	650	54.17	157	276242	F	86135	1	NSY	001		22503
23200000000000D	TRUCK PICKUP	EA	1.00	HX	4200	160.000000	160	3.81	197	276116	F	86014	1	NSV	001		19044
23200000000000D	TRUCK PICKUP	EA	1.00	HX	3430	200.000000	200	5.83	188	276116	F	86014	1	NSV	001		23503
23200000000000D	TRUCK PICKUP	EA	1.00	HX	7242	500.000000	500	6.90	152	276116	F	86014	1	NCE	001		23322

FIGURE 2
USABLE SURPLUS PROPERTY
PERFORMANCE HISTORY REPORT
(TRUCKS)

FIGURE 3
USABLE SURPLUS PROPERTY PERFORMANCE HISTORY REPORT
(STATION WAGONS)

USABLE SURPLUS PROPERTY PERFORMANCE HISTORY REPORT

OPTIONS: FSG =   CL-OF-SUR = 2310A   DRMR =   M/S =   C/C =   SUR/CM-ID =   REPORTING PERIOD: 86043 THRU 87043   PAGE 74

NSN SUR/CM-ID CLASS OF SURP	ITEM NAME	U/I	QTY SOLD	FED C/C	PHY LOC = INVENTORY VALUE	UNIT BID PRICE	SALES PROCEEDS	% RET	ITEM NO.	IFB NO.	M/S	BOD	D/A	PHY LOC	NBR	BDR ID	ZIP CODE
2310004275554A	STATION WAGO	EA	1.00	H9	3800	276.000000	276	7.67	176	276118	L	86007	1	NNS	001		16125
2310004275554A	STATION WAGO	EA	1.00	F8	3450	301.000000	301	8.72	171	276207	L	86084	1	NNS	001		28746
2310004275554A	STATION WAGO	EA	1.00	H9	3234	375.000000	375	11.60	255	316575	F	86205	1	ND	001		39560
2310004275554A	STATION WAGO	EA	1.00	B6	3647	300.000000	300	8.23	177	416453	F	86191	1	AFL	001		98407
2310004275578A	STATION WAGO	EA	1.00	HX	3729	200.000000	200	5.36	142	276094	L	86028	1	ANJ	001		11202
2310004275578A	STATION WAGO	EA	1.00	FX	800	226.000000	226	28.25	110	316208	L	86030	1	NRA	001		00643
2310004501010A	STATION WAGO	EA	1.00	FX	2900	226.000000	226	7.79	235	276325	L	86169	1	FWH	001		64093
2310004501010A	STATION WAGO	EA	1.00	F8	2900	225.000000	225	7.76	221	316302	F	86085	1	FGU	001		36750
2310004501010A	STATION WAGO	EA	1.00	HX	3364	280.000000	280	8.32	266	316247	L	86043	1	FDY	001		79536
2310005317806A	SEDAN	EA	1.00	HX	5616	375.000000	375	6.68	200	276333	F	86191	1	FWP	001		45305
2310005317806A	SEDAN	EA	1.00	F9	6355	210.000000	210	3.30	161	316419	F	86133	1	FH	001		32925
2310005317806A	SEDAN	EA	1.00	F8	6355	175.000000	175	2.75	187	316476	F	86156	1	FH	001		32926
2310005317806A	SEDAN	EA	1.00	H9	6355	300.000000	300	4.72	171	416329	F	86113	1	AFL	001		98272
2310005317806A	SEDAN	EA	1.00	F8	5616	450.000000	450	8.01	243	416384	F	86141	1	FTT	001		94510
2310005317806A	SPORTSWAGON	EA	1.00	F8	6355	800.000000	800	12.59	161	416472	F	86204	1	AFL	001		98407
2310005525874A	SEDAN	EA	1.00	H8	3501	190.000000	190	5.43	202	276214	F	86157	1	NCH	001		29464
2310005525874A	SEDAN	EA	1.00	HX	3240	425.000000	425	13.12	205	276221	F	86086	1	NCH	001		23140
2310005525874A	SEDAN	EA	1.00	F9	3249	75.000000	75	2.31	156	316486	F	86168	1	NAC	001		78363
2310005798942A	SEDAN	EA	1.00	HX	5000	.000000	1	.00	185	315542	F	85241	N	FGU	001		36111
2310005798942A	SEDAN	EA	1.00	HX	5000	60.000000	60	1.20	220	316302	F	86085	1	FGU	001		36054
2310005798942A	SEDAN	EA	1.00	HX	5000	.000000	20	.00	281	316095	L	85318	N	FPM	001		36081
2310005799078A	TRUCK AMBULA	EA	1.00	HX	471	.000000	0	.00	002	416535	F	86240	2	AVO	001		
2310005802729A	STATION WAGO	EA	1.00	HX	2700	200.000000	200	7.41	253	316403	F	86128	1	NCJ	001		28334
2310005802729A	STATION WAGO	EA	1.00	G8	4437	200.000000	200	4.51	155	416168	F	86023	1	ASC	001		
2310005802910A	SEDAN	EA	1.00	H9	6355	70.000000	70	1.10	213	416399	F	86148	1	ASC	001		95205
2310005802919A	SEDAN	EA	1.00	H8	6355	550.000000	550	8.65	094	416261	F	86078	1	FTT	001		95831
2310005802919A	SEDAN	EA	1.00	H9	5615	425.000000	425	7.57	097	416261	F	86078	1	FTT	001		95660
2310008287158A	SEDAN	EA	1.00	HX	3366	121.000000	121	3.59	168	316332	L	86098	1	FKB	001		78214
2310008329907A	TRUCK CARGO	EA	1.00	H9	12924	587.000000	587	4.54	104	316041	B	85330	1	NCJ	005	3000051461	28501
2310008329907A	TRUCK CARGO	EA	1.00	H9	13924	787.000000	787	5.65	106	316041	B	85330	1	NCJ	007	3000051461	28501
2310008329907A	TRUCK CARGO	EA	1.00	H9	13924	787.000000	787	5.65	105	316041	B	85330	1	NCJ	006	3000051461	28501

you want. This is the address to write to for complete information:

> DEFENSE LOGISTICS AGENCY
> Defense Reutilization & Marketing Service
> Federal Center
> 74 North Washington
> Battle Creek, MI 49017-3092

Figure 4 (page 21) is an example of a letter you can use to request information about SPH reports. You'll notice I suggest including your telephone number; agencies will often pick up the phone and resolve their questions right away since it's easier for them than writing letters. More importantly for you, remembering this simple idea could save you literally weeks of lost time.

Now that you've had a glance at the prices paid at auctions, let's start the whole process of making YOU a successful bidder for government surplus. Here is what you will want to do, explained and illustrated step-by-step.

3.2   METHODS OF PURCHASING SURPLUS

Before you jump in with both feet, you'll want to know the different methods the government has for selling its surplus items. Here they are, along with a description of each:

3.2.1   THE SEALED BID

Normally, this method is used to sell large quantities of surplus property having a commercial or technical application which is of interest to divergent buyer groups on a regional or national

FIGURE 4

LETTER REQUESTING SPH REPORT COSTS

(Your address)_____

_____

DEFENSE LOGISTICS AGENCY
Defense Reutilization & Marketing Service
Federal Center
74 North Washington
Battle Creek, MI   49017-3092

Gentlemen:

Please advise my costs to obtain Usable Surplus Property Performance History Reports for the following surplus classes:

_____   (specify the classes you're
                                          interested in; see
_____   Appendix 1)

I am interested in sales made in the past _____ month/year, and in the following geographical areas:

_____

_____

If there is any further information you require or if you have any questions, please contact me at the number which appears below. Thank you.

Very truly yours,

(Your Name)
(Your Telephone Number)

marketing basis. Scrap and recyclable materials are usually sold by this method.

Term sales using this method are employed when property is not immediately available for delivery and is required to be removed as it is generated. The duration of this type of sale usually extends from a 3- to 12-month period. The type of property sold generally consists of waste and scrap of all kinds.

Prospective bidders are notified of such sales by invitations for bid (called "IFBs") in the form of Sales Catalogs. These are similar to the Sales Auction Catalogs described below (see Section 3.3.4). An IFB lists and describes the property for sale, identifies the places where the sale will be held, specifies the conditions under which the property is offered for sale, gives the location of the property, sets forth the inspection and sales dates, and designates the person to contact for further information. IFBs are mailed well in advance of the date of the sale (bid opening date) to allow sufficient time for inspection of the property. The prospective buyers enter the prices they will pay on the bid forms that are also part of the IFB and return the forms to the specified "selling activity" (the military installation conducting the sale) along with the required deposit. The bids are then publicly opened on the specified date of sale. Subsequently, awards are made and the bidders are notified.

3.2.2 THE SPOT BID

Normally, this method is used when there is a variety of commercial type property for which there is a substantial interest and demand in a local market. The prospective buyers inspect the property and submit bids on forms provided by the selling activity. In spot bid sales, buyers must be present at the sale; mailed-in bids are not acceptable. Awards are made to the highest bidder.

3.2.3 RETAIL SALES

Retail sales are conducted at some military installations and offer small quantities of individual items of property at fixed prices based on current market value. For more information about retail sales, contact the DRMR office which serves the geographical area that interests you (see page 23 for DRMR addresses).

3.2.4 AUCTIONS

Auctions are a very popular way of purchasing government surplus. The information on this method is explained quite thoroughly in Section 3.3, **Local Sales Programs.**

3.3 LOCAL SALES PROGRAMS (AUCTIONS)

This program requires the bidder to be physically present at the sale in order to participate. These sales are conducted at facilities throughout the United States and overseas, and generally offer such items as vehicles, typewriters, furniture and office machines, plus personal items such as household appliances, etc. Simply send a postcard to the regional office of the Defense Reutilization and Marketing Region (DRMR) which serves the state or states you are willing to travel to in order to participate (see addresses below). Be sure to write on the postcard the type of item(s) you are interested in buying. That way, if a sale is coming up in your area offering the type of item(s) you want to buy, the government can immediately send you an auction catalog to look over. Write to the following addresses which apply to you:

If you live in or can go to:

Bermuda, Connecticut, Delaware, Greenland, Guantanamo, Illinois, Indiana, Iowa, Kansas, Maine, Maryland, Massachusetts, Michigan, Minnesota, Missouri, Nebraska, New Hampshire, New Jersey, New York, Ohio, Pennsylvania, Rhode Island, Vermont, Virginia, Washington D.C., West Virginia or Wisconsin

Write to: DRMR - COLUMBUS
                       P.O. Box 500
                       Blacklick, OH   43004-0500

If you live in or can go to:

Alabama, Arkansas, Florida, Georgia, Kentucky, Louisiana, Mississippi, New Mexico, North Carolina, Oklahoma, Panama Canal Zone, Puerto Rico, South Carolina, Tennessee or Texas

Write to: DRMR - MEMPHIS
                       P.O. Box 275
                       Memphis, TN   38114-5052
                       (901) 775-6552

If you live in or can go to:

Alaska, Arizona, California, Colorado, Idaho, Montana, Nevada, North Dakota, Oregon, South Dakota, Utah, Washington or Wyoming

Write to: DRMR - OGDEN
P.O. Box 53
Defense Depot Ogden
Ogden, UT 84407-5001

If you live in or can go to:

Azores, Belgium, England, Greece, Iceland, Italy, Spain, Turkey, West Germany

Write to: DRMR - EUROPE
APO NY 09633

(Buyers located <u>outside</u> the United States in the Northern Hemisphere use this address):

          DRMR - EUROPE
Postfach 2027
D6200 Wiesbaden, West Germany

If you live in or can go to:

Guam, Hawaii, Japan, Okinawa, Philippines, South Korea, Thailand

Write to: DRMR SALES OFFICE - PACIFIC
Box 211
Pearl City, HI 96782-0211

If you live in or can go to:

Australia

Write to: DRMR OFFICE - AUSTRALIA
FPO San Francisco, CA 96680-2920

(Buyers located <u>outside</u> the United States in the Southern Hemisphere use this address):

          DRMR OFFICE - AUSTRALIA
U.S. Naval Communications station
Exmouth, Western Australia

Also, refer to Appendix 2 of this directory for a sample listing of locations where sales have historically been held. This will give you a better idea of where sales are, and can show you some of the locations in your general area.

3.3.1 HOW TO GET ON THE BIDDERS MAILING LIST AND RECEIVE FREE AUCTION NOTICES

Being on the Bidders Mailing List will enable you to receive notices of all sales to be held in the geographic locations you wish to attend and which are selling items you are particularly interested in. The first step in getting your name on this list is to inform the DoD of your interest. Address a postcard to:

DoD Surplus Sales
P.O. Box 1370
Battle Creek, MI 49016-1370

On the reverse side of the postcard, print your name and address and a request similar to the following: "Please send me a Department of Defense Surplus Bidder's Application."

Within approximately two weeks you will receive the following documents:

(1) Surplus Property Bidder's Application Form

(2) An instruction booklet entitled "How to Buy Surplus Personal Property from the United States Department of Defense"

I want to stress that this application and instruction booklet are FREE; YOU PAY NOTHING FOR THEM NOW, NOR WILL YOU PAY ANYTHING FOR SENDING IN YOUR APPLICATION ONCE IT IS FILLED OUT.

Now let's take a close look at the "Surplus Property Bidder's Application Form" so you can complete it easily. This form lets you be very specific about what kind of items you are interested in buying, AND what areas you are willing to travel to for purchasing these items. It is very simple to fill out; there are two sides to the form, which are shown in FIGURES 5 and 6 (see pages 27 and 28).

Fill out the name and address information on the top of side 1 of the application form. You'll notice that lines 01 through 33, and lines 42 and 43 contain mostly numbers, divided by rows of alphabetical letters. The numbers represent over **469** major classes of surplus which you can choose from! (A list of these classes are all indexed for you in Appendix 1.) Once you have found the numbers for the items you are interested in, find the same numbers on the application form and circle them.

A special note: Looking at Appendix 1, you will find an incredible array of items! Please select only the items of actual interest to you, or you risk your name being quickly purged from the mailing list! (See more information on "purging" in section 3.3.3 below.)

3.3.2   FINDING AUCTIONS IN YOUR AREA

After you have finished selecting the items you are interested in, look at lines 34 through 41 on side 2 of the application form. These are the locations where surplus sales are held. You may circle as many locations as you are able to attend in person. As you can see from the list, there are 53 regions available, with at least one region in EVERY state, plus Puerto Rico and the Virgin Islands. Therefore, you should have no problem finding an auction within driving distance from your home. After you have circled the appropriate locations, you have completed the application.

Important tip: When filling out your address on the application, be sure to include the last 4 digits in your 9-digit

FIGURE 5
SURPLUS PROPERTY BIDDERS
APPLICATION FORM

DEFENSE REUTILIZATION AND MARKETING SERVICE
DEPARTMENT OF DEFENSE
SURPLUS PROPERTY BIDDERS APPLICATION

NAME *(Firm or Individual) (Last, Blank, First, Blank, Middle)*

ADDRESS

CITY   STATE   ZIP CODE

COMPLETION INSTRUCTIONS:

1. Fill in the blanks provided for your name, address, city, state and zip code.
2. Circle the class number of surplus property in which you are interested and circle the geographical area(s) desired. This will assure that you receive Invitations for Bids only when they contain the property you desire in the specific area you have designated.

(Circle numbers of classes of surplus property desired)

RECYCLABLE MATERIALS *(See pages 13 and 14)*

RSC	A	B	C	D	E	F	G	H	I	J	K	L	M	N	Z
01	8305A	9450A	9450B	9450C	9450D	9450E	9450F	9450G	9660A	9660B	9670C	9670D	9670E	9670F	
02	9670G	9670H	9670J	9670K	9670L	9680B	9680C	9680D	9680E	9680F	9680G	9680H	9680J	9680K	
03	9680L	9680M													

USABLE PROPERTY *(See pages 14 to 40)*

RSC	A	B	C	D	E	F	G	H	I	J	K	L	M	N	Z
04	1005	1190	1220	1240	1260	1265	1270	1280	1285	1290			1440	1450	
05	1510A	1510B	1510C	1520	1550	1560A	1560B	1560C	1610	1615	1620	1630	1650	1660	
06	1670	1680	1710	1720	1730	1740	1940D	2010	2020	2030	2040	2050	2090	2210	
07	2220	2230	2240	2250	2310A	2310B	2310C	2320A	2320B	2320C	2320D	2330	2340	2410	
08	2420	2430	2510	2520	2530	2540	2590	2610	2620	2630	2640	2805	2810	2815	
09	2820	2825	2835	2840	2845	2895	2910	2915	2920	2925	2930	2935	2940	2945	
10	2950	2990	2995	3010	3020	3030	3040	3110	3120	3130	3210	3220	3230	3411	
11	3412	3413	3414	3415	3416	3417	3418	3419	3422	3424	3426	3431	3432	3433	
12	3436	3438	3439	3441	3442	3443	3444	3445	3446	3447	3448	3449	3450	3455	
13	3456	3460	3465	3470	3510	3520	3530	3540	3550	3590	3605	3610	3615	3620	
14	3625	3635	3645	3650	3655	3680	3685	3690	3695	3710	3720	3740	3750	3805	
15	3810	3815	3820	3825	3830	3835	3895	3910	3920	3930	3940	3950	3960	3990	
16	4010	4020	4030	4110	4120	4130	4140	4210	4220	4230	4240	4310	4320	4330	

HQ DRMS Form 340 Jan 86 *(Previous edition to be used until exhausted)*

CONTINUED ON REVERSE

FIGURE 6
SURPLUS PROPERTY BIDDERS
APP. FORM (PAGE TWO)

RSC	A	B	C	D	E	F	G	H	I	J	K	L	M	N	Z
17	4410	4420	4430	4440	4450	4460	4510	4520	4530	4540	4610	4620	4630	4710	
18	4720	4730	4810	4820	4910	4920	4925	4930	4931	4933	4935	4940	4960	5110	
19	5120	5130	5133	5136	5140	5180	5210	5220	5280	5305	5306	5307	5310	5315	
20	5320	5325	5330	5340	5345	5350	5355	5410	5420	5430	5440	5445	5450	5510	

RSC	A	B	C	D	E	F	G	H	I	J	K	L	M	N	Z
21	5610	5640	5650	5660	5670	5680	5805	5815	5820	5821	5825	5826	5830	5831	
22	5835	5840	5841	5845	5895	5905	5910	5915	5920	5925	5930	5935	5940	5945	
23	5950	5955	5960	5961	5965	5970	5975	5977	5985	5990	5995	5999	6105	6110	
24	6115	6120	6125	6130	6135	6140	6145	6150	6210	6220	6230	6240	6250	6320	

RSC	A	B	C	D	E	F	G	H	I	J	K	L	M	N	Z
25	6340	6350	6505	6510	6515	6520	6525	6530	6540	6545	6605	6610	6615	6620	
26	6625	6630	6635	6636	6640	6645	6650	6655	6660	6665	6670	6675	6680	6685	
27	6695	6710	6720	6730	6740	6750	6760	6770	6780	6810	6830	6840	6850	6910	
28	6920	6930	6940	7105	7110	7125	7195	7210	7240	7290	7310	7320	7330	7350	

RSC	A	B	C	D	E	F	G	H	I	J	K	L	M	N	Z
29	7360	7410	7420	7430	7440	7450	7460	7490	7510	7520	7530	7610	7710	7730	
30	7810	7830	7910	7930	8010	8030	8040	8105	8110	8115	8120	8125	8130	8135	
31	8140	8145	8305B	8340	8405	8410	8415	8420	8430	8435	8440	8445	8460	8465	
32	8475	8710	8820	9110	9130	9135	9140	9150	9160	9310	9320	9330	9340	9350	

RSC	A	B	C	D	E	F	G	H	I	J	K	L	M	N	Z
33	9390	9505	9510	9515	9520	9525	9530	9535	9540	9545	9630	9640	9650		

ADPS CODE CJ CK *(For DRMS use only)*

RSC						
34	01 - ALA	02 - ALASKA	03 - ARIZ	04 - ARK	05 - CAL(N)	52 - CAL(S)	06 - COLO
35	07 - CONN	08 - DEL	09 - DC	10 - FLA	11 - GA		13 - IDA
36	14 - ILL	15 - IND	16 - IOWA	17 - KAN	18 - KY	19 - LA	20 - ME
37	21 - MD	22 - MASS	23 - MICH	24 - MINN	25 - MISS	26 - MO	27 - MONT
38	28 - NEBR	29 - NEV	30 - NH	31 - NJ	32 - N MEX	33 - NY	34 - N CAR
39	35 - N DAK	36 - OHIO	37 - OKLA	38 - OREG	39 - PA	40 - RI	41 - S CAR
40	42 - S DAK	43 - TENN	44 - TEX(N)	53 - TEX(S)	45 - UTAH	46 - VT	47 - VA
41	48 - WASH	49 - W VA	50 - WISC	51 - WYO	54 - PUERTO RICO		55 - VIRGIN IS

CLASSES OF SURPLUS SHIPS, PONTOONS, AND FLOATING DOCKS IN WHICH I AM INTERESTED *(Circle numbers of classes desired)*

	A	B	C	D	E	F	G	H	I	J	K	L	M	N	Z
42	1905A	1905B	1905C	1905D	1905E	1905F	1910	1915	1925A	1925B	1925C	1925D	1930A	1930B	
43	1935	1940B	1940C	1945	1950	1990									

FOR ITEMS IN CLASSES 1905A THROUGH 1990 (EXCLUDING CLASS 1940D WHICH IS SELECTED BY STATE), CIRCLE ONLY THE GEOGRAPHICAL AREA(S) PROVIDED.

44	81 - EAST OF MISS RIVER (INCL GULF PORTS)	82 - WORLD-WIDE
	83 - OVERSEAS ONLY	84 - WEST OF MISS RIVER

INDICATE ONE *(Refer to How to Buy pamphlet, page 41)*

☐ SMALL BUSINESS   ☐ LARGE BUSINESS

RETURN THIS APPLICATION TO THE FOLLOWING ADDRESS

DEFENSE REUTILIZATION AND MARKETING SERVICE
P.O. Box 1370
Battle Creek, MI 49016-1370

(zip+4) zip code. You may not realize it, but we ALL have a "zip+4" zip code; if you don't know what yours is, you can easily find out by contacting your local Post Office. If your application does not include the zip+4, IT WILL DELAY THE PROCESSING OF YOUR APPLICATION! Mail your completed application to:

Defense Reutilization & Marketing Service
P.O. Box 1370
Battle Creek, MI 49016-1370

After you have mailed your application, you can expect, within a few weeks, to receive your first auction catalog and pamphlet entitled "SALE BY REFERENCE" which contains standard instructions, terms and conditions normally used in the various methods of surplus sales by the Department of Defense. ALL THIS INFORMATION IS FREE TO YOU!

The "SALE BY REFERENCE" pamphlet also brings you a very important piece of information on the address label: your very own "Bidders Number." Directly to the right of your name you'll find a 10-digit number which you'll use whenever you submit bids in response to Sales Invitations for Bid (called an "IFB"), and in all correspondence concerning the DoD Surplus Sales Program.

As mentioned above, once you are on the mailing list, you'll begin to receive notices of all sales to be held in the geographical areas you chose on your application which are selling the items (from the list of 469 choices) also indicated on your application. Incidentally, if you circled every item (all 469), you can expect to receive loads and loads of catalogs each week! However, **don't do it** ... unless you really ARE interested in everything the Government sells as surplus, for two reasons:

(1) You will be sent several sale notices for EACH item you are interested in, so it's wasteful and abusive of the surplus sales system and resources required for the catalogs; and (2) more importantly, prospective buyers (people like you) who select an excessive number of classes (items) on their application forms and who do not actually buy anything from the sales will be purged -- and **FAST!** What is this purging I keep referring to? Let's briefly discuss it.

3.3.3   THE PURGING OF YOUR NAME

The DoD Surplus Property Bidder's List is continually purged of the names of the people who don't ever make a bid, which is not unreasonable when you remember the costs of all these FREE auction announcements, first-class mailing, etc.

So -- how do YOU keep from being "purged," or removed, from the mailing list?   You'll receive at least 5 auction sales catalogs before you need to worry about being purged; look at your address label on the back of each sales catalog.   When the number "2" appears after your name as follows: @2@, it means you must notify the Defense Surplus Bidder's Control Office that you want to continue to receive auction sales catalogs.   Otherwise, your name will be removed from the Bidder's List.   To notify that office, simply tear out the "CHANGE FORM" of the auction sales catalog (see FIGURE 7 on page 31 for a sample) and mail it to:

> DoD Surplus Sales
> P.O. Box 1370
> Battle Creek, MI   49016-1370

The "CHANGE FORM" may also be used to notify DoD of a change of address, when you wish to discontinue receiving sales catalogs, and to request new Bidder's Application Forms (if you want to add or delete items/areas of interest).

So much for name purging ... we've been asked to explain it on several occasions, so hopefully it is now clear.

3.3.4   THE AUCTION SALES CATALOG

Now let's assume you've received your first auction sales catalog.   Its cover will look similar to the cover shown in FIGURE 8 on page 32.   The cover will usually tell you at a glance:

* The date of the sale
* What types of surplus are for sale
* The sale site and mailing address

In our example, the date of the sale is April 21, 1987.   Trucks, Buses, Trailers, Station Wagons, etc., are for sale, and the sale site is Ogden, Utah.   Note that the sale site is often not at the place where any of the items are located.   In fact, the items grouped for a

FIGURE 7
DEFENSE SURPLUS BIDDERS
CONTROL FORM

BIDDERS CHANGE/REQUEST FORM

COMPLETE THIS FORM AND MAIL ENTIRE PAGE (WITH YOUR ADDRESS LABEL ON THE BACK) TO:

DOD SURPLUS SALES
P. O. BOX 1370
BATTLE CREEK, MICHIGAN 49016

NOTE: **DO NOT MAIL BIDS TO THIS ADDRESS!** BIDS MUST BE SENT TO THE ADDRESS STATED ON THE SALE OF GOVERNMENT PROPERTY — BID AND AWARD PAGE OF EACH SALES CATALOG IN ORDER TO BE PROCESSED.

☐ 1. Continue sending sales catalogs. My Bidder Number is 3000_____.

☐ 2. Discontinue sending sales catalogs.

☐ 3. Change of address (print new address below).

☐ 4. New bidder; send Bidder List application;

NAME_____
ADDRESS_____
CITY_____ STATE_____ ZIP CODE_____
COUNTRY_____

To continue receiving sales catalogs, check ☑ Block No. 1 on the form shown above.

If you no longer wish to receive sales catalogs, check ☑ Block No. 2 on the above form.

To change your address, check ☑ Block No. 3 on the above form and print your new address. Allow four weeks for change to be effected.

NEW BIDDERS — If you wish to be placed on the mailing list to receive sales catalogs, check ☑ Block No. 4 and print your name and address.

IMPORTANT NOTICE TO ALL BIDDERS
CONCERNING RECEIPT OF SALES CATALOGS

Your name may be removed from the active Bidders List for failure to participate. This purge will not occur until you have been forwarded at least 5 sales catalogs and have failed to respond by either submitting a bid or by completing and mailing this form to the address indicated above. This is an on-going purge and requires your attention to assure continued receipt of sales catalogs.

FIGURE 8
AUCTION SALES CATALOG COVER

DEPARTMENT
OF
DEFENSE
DEFENSE REUTILIZATION
AND MARKETING SERVICE

SEALED
BID

41-7248
21 APRIL 1987
9:00 A.M.

SEALED
BID

OFFERING

VEHICLES

AND

COMPONENTS

SALE SITE

FOR SALE SITE AND MAILING
ADDRESS SEE PAGE 61.

particular sale are often located at many different sites in the general area. If you opened up the auction sales catalog in our example, the next page (FIGURE 9, page 34) would show you the locations for the items offered. You'll notice that each location usually has a person's name and telephone number listed for you to call. This is one way the government can keep costs down for the sales; there is no "overhead" of moving many items to the sale site, then returning the ones that didn't sell. If you're interested in the items to be offered, call the contact person to check exactly when you can go and inspect the property. THEN GO SEE IT! Never mind if you don't think it's exactly what you're looking for; if it's of ANY interest, go and see it. You may see other items there which you never realized were available. And, the more you get involved, the more knowledgeable and enthusiastic you'll become.

A typical page from an Auction Sales Catalog is shown in FIGURE 10 on page 35. The item descriptions are quite detailed and include the government's best assessment of condition. These Auction Sales Catalogs make fascinating reading, especially when (as often happens) photographs accompany these descriptions. **READ THE AUCTION SALES CATALOGS YOU RECEIVE FROM COVER TO COVER** -- they will answer a lot of questions for you!

In addition to the Auction Sales Catalogs mailed to you as a potential bidder, notices of sales are often posted in public buildings, advertised on radio, TV and in trade publications, newspapers, etc. Perhaps the best known, and certainly the most comprehensive, is the "Commerce Business Daily"; as its name implies, this is a daily publication put out by the U.S. Department of

FIGURE 9
AUCTION SALES CATALOG —
INSIDE PAGE

IFB 41-7402

DEFENSE REUTILIZATION AND MARKETING REGION
500 WEST 12TH STREET/BLDG. 2A-1
DEFENSE DEPOT OGDEN STATION
OGDEN, UTAH 84407-5001

OFFICE HOURS: (Local Time)   7:00 A.M. to 3:30 P.M.

PRIOR TO BID OPENING DATE: For current and future sales information contact A/C 801, 399-7773. For How to Bid Information contact the Contracting Officer(s) at A/C 801, 399-7462.

AFTER BID OPENING DATE: For High Bid Information which will not be furnished bidders until after awards have been made (See Paragraph 8, Page 1 of Sale by Reference). Payments and Refunds contact A/C 801, 399-7462.

CONTRACTING OFFICER(S):   Contact A/C 801, 399-7462.

PROPERTY LOCATIONS AND CONTACTS

Items 1 thru 71

Defense Reutilization and Marketing Office
Alameda Facility
2155 Mariner Square Loop, Bldg. 5
Alameda, CA 94501-1022
Marketing Branch
Phone: A/C 415, 869-8803

Items 72 thru 75

Defense Reutilization and Marketing Office
Rough and Ready Island
Bldg. 1004
Stockton, CA 95203-4999
Sales Branch
Phone: A/C 209, 944-0267

Items 76 thru 79

Defense Reutilization and Marketing Offsite Branch
Travis Air Force Base
Bldg. 724, Stop 78
Fairfield, CA 94535-7100
Mr. Roger Waring
Phone: A/C 707, 438-3137

Item 80

Ryan Airport
Hemet, CA
Mr. Eugene Fly
Phone: A/C 209, 944-7267

Items 81 thru 143

Defense Reutilization and Marketing Office
McClellan Air Force Base
Sacramento, CA 95652-6448
Mr. Pat Marangi
Phone: A/C 916, 643-3830

Item 144

Defense Reutilization and Marketing Offsite Branch
Mare Island Naval Shipyard
Bldg. 655
Vallejo, CA 94592-5021
Ms. Sharon Fitzgerald
Phone: A/C 707, 646-4368

Items 145 and 146

Defense Reutilization and Marketing Office
Norton Air Force Base, Bldg. 948
San Bernardino, CA 92409-6488
Ms. Vivian Jacqmin
Phone: A/C 714, 382-6164

Items 147 thru 155

Defense Reutilization and Marketing Office
Marine Corps Logistics Base, Bldg. 226
Barstow, CA 92311-5045
Mr. Dan McGowan
Phone: A/C 619, 577-6561

Items 156 thru 168

Defense Reutilization and Marketing Office
Naval Construction Battalion Center, Bldg. 513
Port Hueneme, CA 93043-5015
Mr. M.W. Duran
Phone: A/C 805, 982-5638

Items 169 thru 172

Defense Reutilization and Marketing Office
Outlying Landing Field
P.O. Box 337
Imperial Beach, CA 92032-0337
Mr. Pete Sabanal or Mr. Bud Grover
Phone: A/C 619, 429-0160

Items 173 thru 179

Defense Reutilization and Marketing Offsite Branch
Naval Air Station, North Island
P.O. Box 78
San Diego, CA 92135-5168
Mr. Pete Sabanal or Mr. Bud Grover
Phone: A/C 619, 429-0160

Items 180 thru 189

Defense Reutilization and Marketing Office
Marine Corps Air Station, El Toro
P.O. Box 21
East Irvine, CA 92650-0021
Ms. Sharlene Loper
Phone: A/C 714, 651-4924

FIGURE 10
AUCTION SALES CATALOG
INSIDE PAGE

IFB 41-7248
IT HAS BEEN DETERMINED THAT THIS PROPERTY IS NO LONGER NEEDED BY THE FEDERAL GOVERNMENT.

SEE INSIDE FRONT COVER FOR NAME, ADDRESS, AND TELEPHONE NUMBER OF PERSONS TO CONTACT
FOR FURTHER INFORMATION AND/OR INSPECTION OF PROPERTY LISTED IN THIS IFB.

///
ITEMS 303 THRU 319 ARE LOCATED AT NWC, CHINA LAKE, CA.
///

303. TRUCK, TELEPHONE MAINTENANCE AND CONSTRUCTION: 2½ ton, 1952, The Studebaker Corp., Model M35, Serial M-25017, 6X6, rear duals, tires size 9.00-20, 6 cylinder, REO gasoline engine, equipped with crew compartment and storage compartments, hydraulic boom with Tulsa winch. Parts detached but included transmission, radiator and grill. Parts missing including clutch and pressure plate, steering column, instrument gauges and carburetor.
O/A dim: 268"L X 96"W X 138"H. USN 96-13401.

Outside - Used - Fair Condition
Total Cost: $14,568
Est. Total Wt. 13,000 lbs.

1 EACH

Following Articles Apply if Purchaser elects Option under Note E , Page 59.

AB: Liability and Insurance.
AC: Contract Work Hours and Safety Standards Act-Overtime Compensation.
AD: Convict Labor.
BE: Performance

304. TRUCK, CHASSIS: 2½ ton, 1965, REO Motors Inc., Model SH-S-54, Type M-109, Serial 131972, 6X6, rear duals, tire size 9.00-20, 6 cylinder REO gasoline engine, equipped with Garwood winch, Model CA514-305166, 10,000 lb. capacity. Parts missing including hood, shift lever and alternator. USN 59-00561.

Outside - Used - Fair Condition
Total Cost: $7177
Est. Total Wt. 7000 lbs.

1 EACH

305. TRUCK, TRACTOR, TILT CAB: 1966, IHC, Model VCOF190, Serial 231922G218305, 4X2, rear duals, tire size 9.00-20, V8 gasoline engine. Parts detached but included various engine components.
NSN 2320-00-263-6662. USN 96-18003.

Outside - Used - Poor Condition
Total Cost: $9359
Est. Total Wt. 13,000 lbs.

1 EACH

306. TRUCK, FIRE FIGHTING, AIRCRAFT RESCUE: 500 gl., 1974, Oshkosh Truck Corp., Model MB5A, Serial 13918, 4X4, tire size 15-22.5, Caterpillar, 6 cylinder diesel engine, Model 1673. Parts detached but included fan. NSN 4210-00-216-6618. USN 71-02402.

Outside - Used - Fair Condition
Total Cost: $44,400
Est. Total Wt. 16,000 lbs.

CONTINUED

306. CONTINUED:

1 EACH

O/A dim: 254"L X 97"W X 144"H.

307. TRUCK, CHASSIS: 2½ ton, 1952, Studebaker Corp., Model M-35, Serial M-15720, 6X6, tire size, 9.00-20, 6 cylinder gasoline engine. Parts detached but included drive shaft and third member. Parts missing including instrument panel, drive shaft, front wheels, tires and hubs, 4 ea. rear wheels and tires, radiator, carburetor and approx. back 1/3 of frame.

Outside - Used - Poor Condition
Total Cost: $3255
Est. Total Wt. 7000 lbs.

1 EACH

308. TRUCK, CARGO: 2½ ton, 1951, GMC, Model M135, Serial 2541, 6X6, tire size 11.00-20. Parts detached but included 6 cylinder GMC gasoline engine, radiator and grill work. Parts damaged including windshields and hoods rusted. Parts missing including instrument panel and transmission.
NSN 2320-00-835-8351.

Outside - Used - Poor Condition
Total Cost: $5500
Est. Total Wt. 10,000 lbs.

1 EACH

309. TRUCK, CHASSIS: 2½ ton, 1943, GMC, Model CCKW-353, Serial 258827-2, 6X6, tire size 8.25-20, 6 cylinder gasoline engine, 12 volt electrical system. Parts missing including transmission.

Outside - Used - Fair Condition
Total Cost: $3255
Est. Total Wt. 8000 lbs.

1 EACH

310. TRUCK, CARGO: 5 ton, Kaiser Jeep Corp., Model M54A2W, Serial 5425 11691, 6X6, tire size 11.00-20, equipped with square water tank(Est. dim. of tank 131"L X 95"W X 60"H). Parts missing including engine, radiator, transmission, windshields, front bumper and gauges. NSN 2320-00-055-9265. USN 25-01329.

Outside - Used - Fair Condition
Total Cost: $12,432
Est. Total Wt. 20,000 lbs.

1 EACH

O/A dim: 309"L X 96"W X 120"H.

Commerce. It contains a wealth of information about the daily business of the U.S. Government (your local library should have a copy for you to look at). On the last page of the "Commerce Business Daily" is a list of "SURPLUS PROPERTY SALES"; FIGURE 11 on page 37 shows the back page of the June 4, 1987 issue. You'll notice this particular issue contained notices of sales for used sedans, station wagons, pickups, vans, office machines, miscellaneous electronic equipment and lumber.

If you prefer, you can order your own subscription to the "Commerce Business Daily," but it is quite expensive: $243.00 per year by First Class Mail ($173.00 by Second Class), or $122.00 for 6 months ($87.00 by Second Class). To order, send a check or money order to:

Superintendent of Documents
Government Printing Office
Washington, DC   20402-9371

3.3.5 A DAY AT AN AUCTION

The day of your first auction arrives. You've probably already been to view the items and in your Auction Sales Catalog you've probably made notes about what to bid on and how much it's worth to you. It's a good practice to decide in your mind, BEFORE the auction gets started, what your limit is on any particular item. It's easy to get caught up in the excitement, especially if it's just you and someone else bidding against each other ... you don't want to pay too much just to win the bid!

FIGURE 11
COMMERCE BUSINESS DAILY
(LAST PAGE)

Page 32 COMMERCE BUSINESS DAILY Issue No. PSA-9353 Thursday. June 4, 1987

89 – PEPPER, BLACK, GROUND 18 gm pkt IFB DLA13H-87-B-8343 one award DLA13H-87-C-0852 28.224 mx. $52.183 International Automated Machines INC. 30600 OREGON RD. PERRYSBURG OH 43551-4544.

89 – DESSERT POWDER, PUDDING 8940-00-131-8963 and 8940-00-131-8761 IFB DLA13H-87-B-8055. DLA13H-87-C-0836, P00001. $264.936. one award. 3,920 cs/chocolate, 10,040 cs/vanilla. Continental Mills. 7851 S 192nd St. Kent King WA 98032

89 – BEEF CHUNKS 8925-00-926-6196. IFB DLA13H-87-B-8428 DLA13H-87-C-0853. May 87. $105,480. 36,000 cn Tony Downs Foods Co. 400 Armstrong Blvd N. St James MN 56081.

89 – COOKIE MIX, CHOCOLATE & SUGAR no 10 can IFB DLA13H-87-B-8397. two awards. DLA13H-87-C-0837. 4480 cs/chocolate. 5040 cs/sugar. $127.142 Stellar Industries Inc, 2350 E Devon Ave, Des Plaines IL 60018. Small business. dla13h087-c-08388, 3360 CS/SUGAR. $43,948. Continental Mills Inc, 7851 S 192nd St, Kent King WA 98032.

89 – YELLOW CORNBREAD MIX no 10 can. IFB DLA13H-87-C-0842, 15 May 87. 15,700 cs. $194,662. Stellar Industries Inc, 2350 E Devon Ave, Des Plaines IL 60018.

89 – BLUEBERRY PIE FILLING MIL-P-35029C. IFB DLA13H-87-B-8265. DLA13H-87-C-0856, $677,121, 21,680 cs. Elk Rapids Packing Co. 702 US 31 S. Elk Rapids MI 49629-0128.

Defense Personnel Support Center, 2800 S. 20th St., Philadelphia, PA 19101

89 – PINEAPPLE JUICE 8915-00-634-2439. (DLA13H-87-B-8437) DLA13H-87-C-0096. 6/19/87. 681,233.52. 85,368 cs. 1024,416 cn Maui Pineapple Co. POB 4187 Walnut Creek, CA 94596.

89 – CHILE CON CARNE, DEHY 8940-00-151-6462 MIL-C-43287G. (DLA13H-87-B-8136) DLA13H-87-B-8136. DLA13H-87-C-0805. 15 May 87. $385,624.76. 37,440 cns Right Away Foods Corp, Freeze Dry Div, POB 184, Edinburg, TX 78539.

89 – FLOUR, WHEAT BREAD 10 lb bag and flour. wheat bread. 50 lb bag (DLA13H-87-R-8505) DLA13H-87-C-0869. 21 May 87. 342,000 lb. $53.146 Ross Ind. 715 E 13th St. Wichita. KS 67201. 21 May 87. 925,200 lbs. DLA13H-87-C-0868 $158,102. Intl Multifoods. Multifoods Tower. Minneapolis. MN 55402.

89 – COFFEE, ROASTED, GROUND 2. 3. 20 lb can (DLA13H-87-B-8514) DLA13H-87-C-0872. $470,776. 161,280 lbs. 2 lb can. 96,768 lbs. 3 lb can Wechsler/Richheimer Coffee Corp, 10 Empire Blvd. Moonachie, NJ 07074-1380. DLA13H-87-C-0873. $174,182. 89,600 lbs 20 lb can. Becharas Brothers Coffee Co. 14501 Hamilton. Highland Park, MI 48203.

89 – RELISH, PICKLE, SWEET No 10 can. IFB DLA13H-87-B-8274. DLA13H-87-C-0820. P00001. $59.989 3100 TRK-1. 1120 TPK-2. Bond Food Prod Co. 235 Cook Ave. POB 18. Oconto. WI 54153-0018.

89 – BEANS W/PORK (DLA13H-87-B-8354) DLA13H-87-C-0843 P00001 $88.837 10,560 cs. Milford Canning Co. 300 E Frederick St. Milford IL 60953 DLA13H-87-C-0844 P00001 $50.915 4480 cs. Sandler Fds, POB 396, Norfolk VA 23501

89 – UHT MILK Ft Devens Ft Shafter CID A-A-20113A (DLA13H-87-B-8715) DLA13H-87-C-0864 $87,931. 443 448 Cc Gossner Fds. Inc. 1051 N 10th W. Logan, UT 84321.

99 Miscellaneous

US Army Troop Support Agency, Contracting Group, PO Box 5310, Fort Lee, VA 23801-6020

99 – GROCERY STORE AISLE MARKERS Cont DAHC44-87-C-0016. DAHC44-87-B-0003. Amt $64.455. Dtd 05/01/87. To Cornelius Architectural Products. 30 Pine St Pittsburgh. PA

Defense General Supply Center, Richmond, VA 23297, Tel. 804/275-3350 or 3107

99 – POUCH, HUMAN REMAINS DLA400-87-C-5388 (DLA400-87-B-2815) $122.705 5/14/87 ZAN Machine Co. 59-66 Grand Ave. Maspeth NY 11378-2733

RESEARCH AND DEVELOPMENT SOURCES SOUGHT

In order that potential sources may learn of research and development programs advance notice of the government's interest in a specific research field is published here. Firms having the research and development capabilities described are invited to submit complete information to the purchasing office listed. Information should include the total number of employees and professional qualifications of scientists, engineers, and personnel specially qualified in the R&D area outlined and description of general and special facilities. an outline of previous projects including specific work previously performed or being performed in the listed R&D area; statement regarding industrial security clearance previously granted. and other available descriptive literature. Note that these are not requests for proposals. Respondents will not be notified of the results of the evaluation of the information submitted. but the sources deemed fully qualified will be considered when requests for proposals are solicited. Closing date for submission of responses is 14 days from publication of the notice. unless otherwise specified.

U.S. Nuclear Regulatory Commission Division of Contracts Attn: Yvonne Terry Washington, D.C. 20555

INTEGRATED WASTE PACKAGE EXPERIMENTS (SALT) Poc Cindy Fleenor (301) 492-4741. A performance objective of 10 CFR part 60 for high level waste disposal is containment of the waste for a period of between 300 and 1000 years. At present, the main barrier expected to be used in complying with this requirement is a metallic overpack. Sources are sought for organizations with research capabilities to address uncertainties in 1) synergistic effects in corrosion in bedded salt systems arising from the complexities of realistic corrosion processes as opposed to laboratory tests. 2) scaling and extrapolation of corrosion data from laboratory tests designed to simulate overpack performance in salt, and 3) effects of variability of mineral content in salt overpack behavior in corrosion tests. Organizations must have the following specialized equipment to perform NRC's requirement. 1) corrosion research facilities and equipment. 2) scanning transmission electron microscope. 3) quantitative mineralogical scanning electron microscope equipped for energy-dispersive analysis. and 4) high-intensity. energy-dispersive x-ray defraction device. Interested organizations may send written statements of qualifications to Attention: Cindy Fleenor. Statements are to be submitted for consideration no later than June 9. 1987. See Notes 46 and 68. (153)

U.S. Government Printing Office
Superintendent of Documents
Washington, DC 20402

OFFICIAL BUSINESS
PENALTY FOR PRIVATE USE $300

Postage and Fees Paid
U.S. Government Printing Office
375

FIRST CLASS MAIL

U.S. MAIL

SURPLUS PROPERTY SALES

GSA Federal Supply Service Bureau, Personal Property Services, Sales (6FBPS), 9001 State Line Rd, Rm 307, Kansas City, MO 64114, 816/523-7002

VEHICLES 42 sedans, Chevrolet Citation. Plymouth Reliant. Ford Fairmont, Futura. 1982-84. 7 station wagons, Chevrolet Celebrity Plymouth Reliant 1983-84, 6 hatchbacks, Plymouth Horizon. 1981; 12 vans. Dodge. Ford. Chevrolet. 1980-85. 3 pickups. Dodge. 1980-83 (including crew cab. and 4x4) Special interest: 2 1981 DeLorean coupes. Inspect 8:00 am to 3:30 pm. 22 Jun, and 8:00 am to 9:30 am. 23 Jun. 20th & Leavenworth, Omaha. Auction 9:30 am. 23 Jun. IFB 6FBPS-87-30. (153)

GSA Federal Supply Service Bureau, Personal Property Services, Sales (6FBPS), 9001 State Line Road, Room 307, Kansas City, MO 64114, Tele: (816) 523-7002.

VEHICLES 43 Sedans. Chevrolet Citation. Plymouth Reliant. Ford Fairmont. 1982-84. 5 station wagons. Chevrolet Celebrity. AMC Concord. Plymouth Reliant 1981-84. 2 hatchbacks. Plymouth Horizon. 1981. 2 vans. Dodge. Ford. 1980. 1 pickup. Dodge 1/2 ton. 1980. Inspect 8:00 a.m. to 3:30 p.m., June 23. and 8:00 a.m. to 9:30 a.m., June 24. GSA Fleet Management. Bldg. 87. Fort Des Moines, IA. Auction 9:30 a.m., June 24. IFB 6FBPS-87-32. (153)

Lockheed Missiles & Space Co., Inc., P.O. Box 3504 Sunnyvale, CA 94088-3504, Attn: Pamela Lovett, o/41-20, B/514.

OSCILLOSCOPE, TACHOMETER, CAMERA SCOPE, MISC. ELECTRONIC MATERIAL. Recorder, terminals, filters, hardware, teletypes, wire and cable, misc. test equipment, quench tanks, temperature controller, furnace, inspection machine, manipulator, profilometer, boring and turning machine. Sixteen Items. Acquisition Cost $435,126. Sale Bid Case Number S-5043 Bid Opening Date June 23. 1987. Sale Sealed by Bid. Property Located at Lockheed Warehouse. 227 Curtis Ave., Milpitas CA 95035 Phone (408) 743-8705. Inspection Time 6:00-11:00 AM and 12:00-2:00 PM. (153)

GSA Federal Supply Service Bureau, Personal Property Services, Sales (6FBPS), 9001 State Line Rd, Rm 307, Kansas City, MO 64114, 816/523-7002

MACHINE TOOLS, CLOTHING, INDUSTRIAL EQUIPMENT, ELECTRONIC COMPONENTS & SUPPLIES office machines & furniture, handtools, hardware items, machine tooling, tires, vehicles, and other items. Inspect 8:00 am to 4:00 pm, 23 & 24 Jun, and 8:00 am to 9:00 am, 25 Jun, Iowa Federal Surplus Property Unit, Complex, Fairgrounds, Des Moines. Auction 9:00 am, 25 Jun. IFB 6FBPS-87-28. (153)

Rockwell International, 12214 Lakewood Blvd, Downey, CA 90241. Mary Peterson, Supervisor, Surplus Sales, 213/922-3444

SCRAP Inconel 718 nickel base forgings. Used in making the latches of the space shuttle payload bay doors. Weight approx 11,000 lbs. Est acquisition cost $735,846. Bid Invitation No. 8706-S-C-10. Date of bid opening: 6/25/87. Type of sale: sealed bid. Location of property: Rockwell International, 12214 Lakewood Blvd, Downey, CA. Bldg 19, Surplus Sales. (153)

GSA, Federal Supply Service Bureau, Property Management Branch, Sales (7FBPS), 819 Taylor St., Fort Worth, TX. 76102, Tele: (817) 334-2352.

SEDANS, 1986 LINCOLN TOWN CAR, PICKUPS, OFFICE FURNITURE, OFFICE MACHINES AND EQUIPMENT, MEDICAL EQUIPMENT, And others. Sealed Bid Sale 7FBS-87-72. Inspection is June 15-19, 1987. Bids will be opened June 24, 1987, in Fort Worth, TX. (153)

Defense Reutilization & Marketing Region, Dept. CBD, P.O. Box 500 Blacklick, OH 43004-0500, Phone: A/C 614 238-2114

VEHICULAR & VEHICULAR COMPONENTS Invitation 27-7363. Bid Opening Date 7 Jul 87. Property Location: ME. RI. NY. NJ. PA. MD. VA. OH. MI. IL. WI. KS. NE (153)

Description of Legend

❶ The Procurement item is 100 percent set aside for small business concerns.

❷ A partial quantity or a portion of the procurement item is set aside for small or minority business concerns.

❸ The contract is a labor surplus area set-aside under the provisions of Defense Manpower Policy No. 4B.

❹ Notices of intention to purchase which are published before the IFB's are issued directly to those requesting the proposal.

❺ The procurement will be made in accordance with either DAR part 5, part 501 (Military agencies) or FPR part 1-2, paragraph 12.500 (Civil agencies) and is the first step of a two-step formally advertised procurement. Only those firms submitting qualified responses on the first step will receive notifications when the purchase is made.

★ This synopsis is published for information purposes to alert potential subcontractors and/or suppliers of the proposed procurement. Additional proposals are not solicited.

NUMBERED NOTES are published only on the first working day of each week. The pages containing the "notes" should be retained for reference.

JULIAN DATE — E.G. (000). The number in parenthesis is the Julian Date indicating when this item was edited. It is not part of the synopsis.

SUBSCRIPTION INFORMATION

$243 a year (First Class mailing). $173 a year (Second Class mailing).
6 Month Trial Subscription $122 (First Class), $87 (Second Class)
Foreign Rate $215.25 a year. $108.75 six months, plus Air Mail rates
Two year subscription available at above yearly rates

To Order. Send remittance with full mailing address to the Superintendent of Documents, Government Printing Office. Washington, DC 20402-9371. Tel. 202/783-3238. Purchase order must be accompanied by payment. Make check payable to Superintendent of Documents. Visa, Master Charge, or Choice also acceptable. Allow Approximately 6 weeks for delivery of first issue.

Service problems. Call Superintendent of Documents, Government Printing Office. Washington, DC Tel. 202/275-3054.

Expiration. Subscriptions expire one year from the date of the first issue. One expiration notice is mailed about 90 days before expiration date.

Address Changes. Send to Superintendent of Documents. Government Printing Office, Washington, DC 20402-9373, with entire mailing label from last issue received.

EDITORIAL RESPONSIBILITY

The U.S. Department of Commerce (CBD), Room 1304, 433 W. Van Buren, Chicago, IL 60607, is responsible for compilation and editing only. Tel: FTS 8/353-2950 COM 312/353-2950. Teletype Routing Indicator RUCHODY, or Telex TTY 62875619. (See note 83)

U.S. GOVERNMENT PRINTING OFFICE 1987—807-[illegible]

At an auction you'll meet a cross-section of the public -- everyone and anyone. There will be several dealers (which is always a good sign, because they can recognize a good sale); this means there are lots of bargains available!

At the appointed hour (noted on your Auction Sales Catalog), the government auctioneer will go to work. He will probably spend the first fifteen minutes or so explaining the rules of the sale. You'll normally bid by raising a card that has your number on it, although there are dozens of variations. Even if you don't buy anything, it can be very entertaining to watch the people and see how they react ... especially when bidding gets down to two people who want the same item!

3.3.6 TIPS FOR BIDDERS

Here are some good tips listed by the Government in its "Sale by Reference" pamphlet.

1. **Review the terms and conditions of each sale carefully.** If you have questions, consult the Contracting Officer at the sales office.

2. Don't bid for more material than you can pay for and remove within the removal time allowed. Overbuying may result in forfeiture of your bid deposit or assessment of storage charges.

3. Be sure your bid is "responsive." Bids are solicited on many different units of measure; i.e., pound, foot, each, ton. Be sure your bid responds to the proper unit of measure.

4. Always verify your unit price and your total price before signing and mailing a sealed bid. Mistakes can prove costly to you and will delay processing your bid. Put your initials by any erasures and changes made on your bid.

5. Be sure to address your bid to **the exact mailing address given in the sales catalog.** CAUTION: Do <u>NOT</u> mail bids to DoD Surplus Sales at P.O. Box 1370, Battle Creek, Michigan.

6.   Mail your bid early to allow extra time for postal handling.

7.   Your bid envelope must contain:

* Your complete return address (always use same name and address as on bid form)

* The sale number, opening date and time

* Your bidder I.D. number, if one has been assigned

The above insures processing your bid expeditiously, assures proper credit for your participation in these sales, and precludes opening sealed bids for identification.

So now you've been to an auction ... what's next? Well, let's suppose you'd like a list of successful bidders at either the auction you attended (and didn't bid at) or one you didn't attend but have the Sales Auction Catalog for. Here's what you do:

3.3.7 HOW TO GET FREE LISTS OF SUCCESSFUL BIDDERS

Simply send a postcard requesting a List of Successful Bidders for Sale No. XX-XXXX to the DRMR office which conducted the sale (see page 23 for addresses).

If you went to an auction and made an unsuccessful bid, you will automatically receive this list of successful bidders. On all other occasions you should write for it. This list gives you an enormous amount of additional useful information -- FREE! (NOTE: Hang on to your Auction Sales Catalog after the auction; it will help you when you get the list.) This information will help you to better understand how much is likely to be paid for which items. However, remember that no two sales are exactly alike; many unpredictable factors dictate the number of people who show up and the prices they pay. Perhaps this story from the Washington Navy Yard will illustrate the point:

"... One of the best (worst from your point of view) days the Washington Navy Yard ever had was during a blizzard that dropped 6 inches of snow on the ground. More than 500 bidders showed up because they thought everyone else would stay home! ..."

We've reduced portions of a typical Successful Bidders List in FIGURE 12 (page 41). It shows the bidder's number, the Sales Auction Catalog number he or she bid on (check against description in your own catalog that you saved after the sale), and how much he or she paid. By always getting and checking these lists, you can quickly get a feel for prices and decide on a buying "game plan." If you want to get all possible information, you can also request the Surplus Property Performance History Reports (SPH Reports, discussed in Section 3.1 on page 10) to help you spot prices, location, impact, etc.

3.4   REVIEW

Let's see what we've covered so far:

* You've learned about the HISTORY (SPH) REPORTS and how to get them
* You've been put on the Bidder's List
* You've started to get the Auction Sales Catalogs
* You've learned about finding and reviewing sale items before the auction
* You've learned about the "Commerce Business Daily"
* You're -- hopefully -- beginning to realize what an incredible range of bargains there are if you just look for them!

FIGURE 12
SUCCESSFUL BIDDERS LIST

PAGE NO.   5

IFB NO.   27-9163

NAME AND ADDRESS	BRN	ITEM NO.	ITEM NAME	U/I		UNIT-PR-BID
GARY LEE LENTZ	231	269	TRK PANEL	17 37	EA	337.00
HAYDEN AUTO SVC	236	224	TRK VAN	17 37	EA	325.00
		225	TRK VAN	17 37	EA	325.00
		226	TRK VAN	17 37	EA	325.00
		232	TRK VAN	17 37	EA	475.00
		237	TRK VAN	17 37	EA	325.00
RICHARD EARL MAHAN	238	003	SEDAN	57 26	EA	78.85
A ALWEIS	241	164	TRK AMBULANCE	17	EA	269.73
WILLIAM C CHRISTMAN	247	286	TRK STK&PLTFRM	57 37	EA	2025.00
BRANCHVILLE SALVAGE CO	250	130	TRAILER CARGO	17	EA	251.00
		131	TRAILER CARGO	17	EA	261.00
HARRY J HART	252	207	TRK STK&PLTFRM	17 37	EA	2100.00
EVANS AUTO SALES	257	206	TRK TRACTOR	17 36	EA	377.00
		210	TRK TRACTOR	17 36	EA	305.00
		221	TRK VAN	17 36	EA	1220.00
		259	SEMITRAILER STK	17 33	EA	375.00
V H MCDOW&SON SALVAGE	260	014	PICKUP	17 37	EA	225.14
		075	PICKUP	17 37	EA	175.75
		077	PICKUP		EA	177.77

3.5   WHERE ARE THE JEEPS?

No discussion about DoD Surplus ("Military Surplus") would be complete without a few words about surplus jeeps!   We've all heard stories about people buying surplus military jeeps at incredibly low prices ... jeeps for $38.00 and the like.   Well, these stories are more fiction than fact.   Here are some of the facts about buying surplus jeeps from the DoD, taken from their "Surplus Jeep Fact Sheet":

1.   Kinds of jeeps available: M-151 Series (M-151, M151A1, M151A2, M718, M825).   Almost all military jeeps currently in use are of the M-151 series.   The M-151 has a rear suspension system designed specifically for off-road use.   When driven on pavement, the M-151 has a dangerous tendency to roll over without warning.   Therefore, in the interest of public safety, the Federal Government has a long-standing policy of not selling M-151s as driveable vehicles.   When an M-151 is sold, the buyer is allowed to remove usable components such as the engine, seats, wheels and axles.   **The unitized body of the jeep must then be crushed or cut into four pieces before it is removed by the buyer.**

2.   M-38 Series (military) and CJ-Series (civilian, CJ-3, CJ-5, etc.): Unlike the M-151, these jeeps ARE available in as-is condition. THEY ARE VERY RARE IN MILITARY USE, HOWEVER.

3.   The price jeeps sell for: This varies, of course, depending upon condition, age and location.   The residue of an M-151 jeep, with the unitized body destroyed as described in paragraph 1 above, still often sells for more than $100.   Usable jeeps such as CJ-5s often sell for $1,000 or more.

The bottom line, then, is that most military jeeps (M-151 Series) are cut up into four pieces before you can remove them from the auction site -- good for parts but not very good transportation!   Do watch for jeeps of the M-38 and CJ Series ... they are rare, but how many jeeps do you need?!

Keep in mind that the Department of Defense only handles military jeeps (and other property); **there are other excellent sources for buying Government surplus jeeps,** which are covered on the following pages.

4.0   BUYING FROM THE GENERAL SERVICES ADMINISTRATION

While the Department of Defense handles all of the Government's surplus military property, the GSA handles the procurement and disposition of just about all other Government property.   GSA buys most furnishings, office equipment and supplies used in government offices across the country, along with cars, trucks, tractors, jeeps and other vehicles used by Government employees.

When a Government agency discards a still-usable piece of property, it is returned to GSA.   If no other Government agency wishes to purchase the property, it is sold to the general public.   You'll find a tremendous variety of items in GSA sales.   For example, in a recent sale (Sale No. 09FBPS7030), GSA offered the following items to the general public: electric typewriters, calculators, telephone answering devices, (5) 1980 Cheverolet pickups, 1976 Chevrolet van, 1978 Station wagon, 1977 Clark Forklift, 29 passenger bus, computer equipment, Willys Jeep, desks, X-Ray machine, Wheelchair, and auto repair equipment.   And these are just **a few samples** selected from the hundreds of items listed in the sale notice.   See FIGURE 13 on page 44, which is a copy of a page from GSA's sale catalog from this sale.

4.1   DRUG ENFORCEMENT ADMINISTRATION SEIZURES

Here's where GSA gets some of the most interesting property it sells to the general public.   DEA (Drug Enforcement Administration) seizures account for a tremendous amount of unusual property found in GSA sales. Here's how it works: When people are arrested for selling illegal drugs, the law entitles the Government to seize all property which is even remotely connected to these activities.   All property used (or intended for use) to transport the illegal substances (including aircraft, vehicles and boats), all property which is used as a container for the illegal substance(s) and **all other things of value furnished by any person in exchange for an illegal substance in violation of the law** are confiscated.

Also, since the proceeds of any exchange of illegal substances must be forfeited to the Government, **any property which was purchased with the proceeds must also be forfeited** -- and this includes **everything** -- cars, homes, jewelry, boats, stereos, furs.   You name it, the Government has seized it!

FIGURE 13
GSA SALE CATALOG

LOT	DESCRIPTION	QUANTITY	LOT	DESCRIPTION	QUANTITY
	THE FOLLOWING LOTS ARE LOCATED AT: DEPARTMENT OF JUSTICE INS U.S. BORDER PATROL BUILDING 312 CAMP PARK PLEASANTON CA 94566 CUSTODIAN: KEN SUMMERS PHONE NO: 415-828-3770 X0000 FTS NO: 000-000-0000 BIDDERS MUST CALL FOR APPOINTMENT TO INSPECT AND REMOVE		026	PALLET MOVER: 1975 BARRETT, MDL. SGX-40-28-72, 4000 LB. CAP, S/N 16-32146, HARTNER 220/400V BATTERY CHARGER, W/O BATTERY CHARGER. (HX7WDW6066 #0006)	1 EA
019	STATION WAGON: 1978 CHEVROLET, 8 CYL., AT, PS, AC, S/N 1N35L8J242013. EXTENSIVE REPAIRS REQUIRED. (SPD. 274-86-5869 1591B17009 #0001)	1 EA		THE FOLLOWING LOTS ARE LOCATED AT: DEPARTMENT OF THE INTERIOR BUREAU OF RECLAMATION SHASTA DAM OFFICE (CVP) REDDING CA 960039445 CUSTODIAN: SALLY A. CROWELL PHONE NO: 916-275-3091 X0000 FTS NO: 000-000-0000 BIDDERS MUST CALL FOR APPOINTMENT TO INSPECT AND REMOVE	
020	VAN: 1976 CHEVROLET, 8 CYL., AT, PS, S/N CGL256U-132475. EXTENSIVE REPAIRS REQUIRED. (SPD. 274-86-5912 1591B17009 #0002)	1 EA	027	MISCELLANEOUS ELECTRICAL EQUIPMENT: CONSISTING OF: 1 EA. CIRCUIT BREAKER CABINET, TWO BREAKER ENCLOSURE, TYPE AT, 6.9KV G.E. DWG. K6560152-1, AT-INLINE COMPLETER W/ CONTROL SWITCHES & OVERCURRENT RELAYS; CONTAINS ONE CIRCUIT BREAKER, OIL BLAST, G. E. K6560152-104 TYPE FK255-150, 15000 VOLT, 600 AMP., 1 EA. SWITCH, DISCONNECT, INDOOR, TYPE ATCOMPT, 13,200 VOLT, 1250 KVA GE K6560319; 12 EA. TRANSFORMERS, ELECT., 200 KVA ALLIS CHAMBERS, TYPE CB, 60 CYCLES, SINGLE PHASE, HIGH VOLTAGE, 2280/2520, LOW VOLTAGE 480, INSULATED FOR Y CONNECTION, 110 GALLON OIL CAPACITY, S/N'S 1762101-12; 6 EA. TRANSFORMERS, ELECT., 10 KVA, TECH TRAN CO., SINGLE PHASE PRIMARY VOLT 7960, SECONDARY VOLTS 120/240 TYPE CP; 2 EA. CURRENT LIMITING REACTOR, TRENCH ELECT., 3 PHASE (2 EA. BANKS) IMPEDANCE 1.25 OHMS AT 60 HZ, VOLTAGE RATING 7,200 VOLT, BASIC INSULATION LEVEL, 95 KILOVOLTS, CONTINUOUS CURRENT RATING 125 AMP, VOLTAGE DROP 156 VOLTS AT 60 HZ RATED KVA 19.5 KVA PER PHASE, TYPE INDOOR DRY TYPE, SELF-COOLED 60 HZ SHORT CIRCUIT W/STAND CAPABILITY, 4.166 AMP, RMS SYMMETRICAL. NOTE: TWO 3-PHASE CURRENT LIMITING REACTOR BANKS UN-ASSEMBLED, ANSI C57.16 PRODUCTION TESTS, A/C $67,245. (1491N36139 #1001-4 & 1491N36118 #1001)	1 LOT
021	SEDAN: 1966 BUICK, 8 CYL., AT, PS, PB, S/N 48239H-160187. EXTENSIVE REPAIRS REQUIRED. (SPD. 274-86-6234 1591B17009 #003)	1 EA			
	THE FOLLOWING LOTS ARE LOCATED AT: ARMY/AIR FORCE EXCHANGE SERV OAKLAND ARMY BASE BUILDING 99 OAKLAND CA 94626 CUSTODIAN: SCOTT TAYLOR PHONE NO: 415-466-2377 X0000 FTS NO: 000-000-0000 BIDDERS MUST CALL FOR APPOINTMENT TO INSPECT AND REMOVE				
022	PICKUP: 1978 CHEVROLET LUV, 4 CYL., MT, S/N CLN1488252222. REPAIRS REQUIRED: CLUTCH. (HX7WDW6321 #0001)	1 EA	028	CLEANER: STEAM & PARTS WASHER, JENNY MDL. 1000-C 125 PSI, 2.5 GPM, BRIGGS & STRATTON GAS ENGINE, 8HD PUMP 4 GPM 15.2 1/MIN., 1070 RPM, MAX. 1200 PSI, 160 DEGREES F, 1980 MFG. YR., EST. WT. 450 LBS. REPAIRS REQUIRED: TANK NEEDS REPLACEMENT. (1491N36188 #1003)	1 EA
023	FORKLIFT: NARROW AISLE ELECT., CONSISTING OF: STANDUP RIDER, 1977 CLARK, S/N'S NST245993630FA & NST245983630FA; 1 EA. 36 VOLT STANDUP RIDER REACH, 1975 RAYMOND, S/N 031DDR30TT4509. EXTENSIVE REPAIRS REQUIRED: ELECT., DRIVE UNIT, SPINDLE BRACKET, CASTER WHEEL, LOWERING HANDLE. (HX7WDW-6321 #0002,0003,0005)	1 EA		5TH & OAK STREETS WAREHOUSE SUSANVILLE CA 96130 CUSTODIAN: WILLIAM WHITSON PHONE NO: 916-257-2151 X0000 FTS NO: 000-000-0000	
024	FORKLIFT: SITDOWN, 1976 CLARK MDL. EC30025, 36V, 2000 LB. CAP, S/N EC236352703FA. REPAIRS REQUIRED: STEER AXLE W/O BATTERY OR CHARGER. (HX7WDW6028 #2)	1 EA	064	WHEELCHAIR: ELEVATOR, MDL. B-42, 350-LB. MAX. LOAD, 48" MAX. LIFT, S/N 6972. (129JNE6037 #1)	1 EA
057	PICKUP: 1980 CHEVROLET LUV, 4 CYL., 4 SPD. MT, 4WD, S/N CRN14A8248157, WITH CAMPER SHELL. REPAIRS REQUIRED. (1482VF6283 #68 1482VF6281)	1 EA		THE FOLLOWING LOTS ARE LOCATED AT: DEPARTMENT OF THE INTERIOR BUREAU OF LAND MANAGEMENT 705 HALL STREET SUSANVILLE CA 96130 CUSTODIAN: KAREN PACKWOOD PHONE NO: 916-257-5385 X0000 FTS NO: 000-000-0000 BIDDERS MUST CALL FOR APPOINTMENT TO INSPECT AND REMOVE	
058	PICKUP: 1980 CHEVROLET LUV, 4 CYL., 4 SPD. MT, S/N CRN14A8285824. REPAIRS REQUIRED: ENGINE. LONG STORAGE. (1482VF6283 #69 1482VF6281)	1 EA	065	PICKUP: 1981 DODGE, 8 CYL., 4 SPD. MT, 4WD, PS, PB, S/N 1B7KW24R1BS72220. REPAIRS REQUIRED. (1482VF6283 #7802 1482VF6282)	1 EA
059	PICKUP: 1980 CHEVROLET LUV, 4 CYL., 4 SPD. MT, 4WD, S/N CRN14A8273537. INOPERABLE: Engine. (1482VF6283 #70 1482VF6281)	1 EA	066	PICKUP: 1981 DODGE, 8 CYL., AT, PS, PB, S/N 1B7HW14R4BS168876. REPAIRS REQUIRED. (1482VF6283 #7801 1482VF6282)	1 EA
060	PICKUP: 1980 CHEVROLET LUV, 4 CYL., 4 SPD. MT, 4WD, S/N CRN14A8249981. REPAIRS REQUIRED: CLUTCH, GRILL & 1 HEADLIGHT MISSING. LONG STORAGE. (1482VF6283 #71 1482VF6281)	1 EA	067	VAN: 1980 DODGE, 8 CYL., AT, PS, PB, S/N B31KTAX-121722. REPAIRS REQUIRED. (1482VF6283 #7800 1482VF6282) W/4WD	1 EA
	THE FOLLOWING LOTS ARE LOCATED AT: DEPARTMENT OF THE INTERIOR BUREAU OF LAND MANAGEMENT 555 LESLIE STREET UKIAH CA 95482 CUSTODIAN: CATHY PRATT PHONE NO: 707-462-3873 X0000 FTS NO: 000-000-0000			THE FOLLOWING LOTS ARE LOCATED AT: DOT IRS WAREHOUSE DOOR 25 1070 SAN MATEO AVENUE SOUTH SAN FRANCISCO CA 94080 CUSTODIAN: SHIRLEY GALLAGHER (SAN FRAN.) PHONE NO: 415-556-2479 X0000 FTS NO: 000-000-0000 BIDDERS MUST CALL FOR APPOINTMENT TO INSPECT AND REMOVE	
061	PICKUP: 1980 CHEVROLET LUV, 4 CYL., 4 SPD. MT, S/N CLN1448208490. REPAIRS REQUIRED. (1482VF6283 #80 1482VF8280)	1 EA	068	MISCELLANEOUS OFFICE MACHINES: INCLUDING: TRANSCRIBERS, CALCULATORS, TELEPHONE DICTATION MACHINES, CASH REGISTERS, COPY MACHINES, ACCOUNTING MACHINES, MICROFILM & MICROFISHE READER/PRINTER, DICTAPHONE, MAIL SEALERS & OPENERS, TAPE RECORDER, SLIDE PROJECTORS, TALLYPRINTER, FILM STRIP PROJECTORS, DICTATION MACHINE. REPAIRS REQUIRED. (2091256328 #1 THRU 28; -6335 #11 THRU 15; -6150 #1, 2, 4 & 5)	1 LOT
062	PICKUP: 1979 TOYOTA, 4 CYL., 4 SPD. MT, S/N RN32023207. REPAIRS REQUIRED. (1482VF6283 #79 1482VF86280)	1 EA			
	THE FOLLOWING LOTS ARE LOCATED AT: DEPARTMENT OF THE INTERIOR BUREAU OF RECLAMATION MOUNTAIN HOUSE & KELSO ROADS TRACY CA 95376 CUSTODIAN: DORIS ECKHARDT PHONE NO: 209-836-6246 X0000 FTS NO: 000-000-0000				
063	MISCELLANEOUS PROPERTY: INCLUDING: BATTERY CHARGER; AMMETER; CALCULATORS; MULTIMETER; TESTERS; INDICATOR; WATTMETERS; VOLTMETERS; MILAMMETERS; TACHOMETER. EXTENSIVE REPAIRS REQUIRED. 1491N36237 #2001 THRU 2018)	1 LOT			

As you can imagine, these seizures produce some pretty luxurious items, most of which are later sold by the GSA. If you've heard of people buying exotic cars like Ferraris or expensive jewelry at Government auctions, this is probably where the property came from. Whatever your needs or wants, the Government can undoubtedly provide what you're looking for. If you don't believe it, take a look at a few of the "typical" items listed in a recent U.S. Department of Justice DEA Notice of Seizure published in the popular newspaper "USA Today":

Seizure No.	Item
9511	1977 Porsche Targa
10680	1981 BMW 733I
10853	1986 Porsche 911
9035	1985 Mercedes Benz 190E
9779	1978 Mercedes Benz 280SL
10753	1985 Cadillac Eldorado
10483	Gulfstream Aircommander
10154	1969 Piper Navajo
10968	Rolex Watch
10242	5 Fur Coats
9290	1 Story Brick House
9023	1 Story Brick and Wood House
10725	House Trailer
10589	Sony Home Video Recorder
10712	1985 Honda Motorcycle

Remember, theses are just a few examples of the types of items which are confiscated and are eventually turned over to GSA to be sold to the general public. These particular examples were chosen from a notice containing **HUNDREDS** of other similar items. The point is, new items become part of GSA's inventory due to drug seizures almost every day. If you keep your eyes open, you can find some truly unusual bargains!

4.2   HOW TO BUY SURPLUS AND CONFISCATED PROPERTY FROM GSA

The first step, as you might have already guessed, is to get on GSA's mailing list. GSA sales are conducted through 11 GSA regional Customer Service Bureaus across the country. Choose the geographical area(s) you're interested in from the list below and send a postcard to **each** regional office which handles those area(s). Here's a sample of how your postcard might read:

Gentlemen:

Please send me a Surplus Personal Property Mailing List application and any additional information you have concerning GSA Surplus Sales.

Thank you.

(Your Name)
(Your Complete Address)

GSA Regional Customer Service Bureau Addresses

REGION 1

10 Causeway Street, 9th Floor
Boston, MA   02222

Areas Served: Connecticut, Maine, Massachusetts, New Hampshire, Rhode Island, and Vermont

REGION 2

General Services Administration
26 Federal Plaza
New York, NY   10278

Areas Served: New Jersey, New York, Puerto Rico and Virgin Islands

REGION 3

General Services Administration
Ninth and Market Streets
Philadelphia, PA   19107

Areas Served: Delaware, Maryland, Virginia (except Washington DC metropolitan area), Pennsylvania and West Virginia

REGION 4

General Services Administration
75 Spring Street
Atlanta, GA   30303

Areas Served: Alabama, Florida, Georgia, Kentucky, Mississippi, North Carolina, South Carolina and Tennessee

REGION 5

General Services Administration
230 South Dearborn Street
Chicago, IL   60604

Areas Served: Illinois, Indiana, Michigan, Minnesota, Ohio and Wisconsin

REGION 6

General Services Administration
4400 College Blvd., Suite 175
Overland Park, KS   66211

Areas Served: Iowa, Kansas, Missouri and Nebraska

REGION 7

General Services Administration
819 Taylor Street
Fort Worth, TX   76102

Areas Served: Arkansas, Louisiana, New Mexico, Oklahoma and Texas

REGION 8

General Services Administration
Building 41-Denver; Federal Center
PO Box 25506
Denver, CO   80225-0506

Areas Served: Colorado, Montana, North Dakota, South Dakota, Utah and Wyoming

REGION 9

General Services Administration
525 Market Street
San Francisco, CA   94105

Areas Served: Arizona, California, Commonwealth of the Northern Mariana Islands, Guam, Hawaii, and Nevada

REGION 10

General Services Administration
GSA Center
Auburn, WA 98002

Areas Served: Alaska, Idaho, Oregon and Washington

NATIONAL CAPITAL REGION

General Services Administration
7th & D Streets, SW
Washington, DC 20407

Areas Served: Washington DC metropolitan area and nearby Maryland and Virginia

You should receive your "Surplus Personal Property Mailing Application" in four to six weeks. See FIGURE 14 on page 49 for a sample of a GSA Application for Region 4. Let's go through the application section by section:

Section 1: Fill in your name and address. Print carefully.

Section 2: Mark "X" in the box next to each geographical area you're interested in. (Remember -- it's a good idea to mark ONLY those areas in which you really plan to bid; if you mark all areas, your name will be quickly purged from the mailing list if you don't bid in all areas you chose.)

Sections 3 and 4: Mark "X" in blocks for the type of property you're interested in. See below for Codes and Descriptions. Again, be sure to mark only those classes of surplus property in which you have a serious interest. Applicants who mark all (or most) of the 27 boxes are assumed to be "lookie-lou's" and are quickly removed from the mailing list.

USABLE PROPERTY SUPPLIES & EQUIPMENT
CODES AND DESCRIPTIONS

0001   Aircraft, Aircraft Engines and Parts
0002   Motor Vehicles, Equipment and Parts
0003   Boats and Marine Equipment
0004   Chemicals, Fuels, Oils, Paints, Sealers and Waxes
0005   Clothing, Textile and Leather Groups
0006   Construction and Building Materials

FIGURE 14
GSA SURPLUS PERSONAL PROPERTY
MAILING APPLICATION

NOTE: FORMS DATED PRIOR TO NOVEMBER 1986 ARE OBSOLETE AND WILL NOT BE ACCEPTED

GSA FORM 2170 (REV. 11-86)	**SURPLUS PERSONAL PROPERTY MAILING LIST APPLICATION**	OMB APPROVED NO. 3090-0023

BIDDER MUST COMPLETE AS APPLICABLE

INDICATE ADDRESS ACTION | **PROPERTY CHANGES** |

☐ NEW ☐ CHANGE | ☐ ADD ☐ DELETE |

NAME (Last, first, middle initial)

ADDRESS

CITY, STATE, ZIP CODE

GEOGRAPHIC AREAS OF BIDDING INTEREST
(Mark "X" in the block(s) in which you have an interest) ☐ ALL LOCATIONS LISTED BELOW EXCEPT HAWAII

1 ☐ HOLBROOK, AZ (S1)	6 ☐ FRESNO, CA (S6)	11 ☐ SAN DIEGO, CA (SB)
2 ☐ PHOENIX, AZ (S2)	7 ☐ SACRAMENTO, CA (S7)	12 ☐ SANTA MARIA, CA (SC)
3 ☐ TUCSON, AZ (S3)	8 ☐ S.F. BAY AREA (S8)	13 ☐ HAWAII (SD)
4 ☐ YUMA, AZ (S4)	9 ☐ REDDING, CA (S9)	14 ☐ LAS VEGAS, NV (SE)
5 ☐ EDWARDS, CA (S5)	10 ☐ LOS ANGELES, CA (SA)	15 ☐ RENO, NV (SF)

USABLE AND RECYCLABLE PROPERTY
(Mark "X" in the block(s) in which you have an interest)

USABLE PERSONAL PROPERTY

☐ AMMUNITION CASINGS, RELOADABLE (Restricted to Licensed Dealers) (13)
☐ AIRCRAFT (Includes: Engines, Parts, Accessories and Support Equipment) (15)
☐ BOATS AND MARINE EQUIPMENT (19)
☐ RAILROAD EQUIPMENT (22)
☐ MOTOR VEHICLES, TRAILERS, CYCLES, AND SNOWMOBILES (23)
☐ CONSTRUCTION, MINING, EXCAVATING, AND HIGHWAY MAINTENANCE EQUIPMENT (24)
☐ MANUFACTURING MACHINERY, EQUIPMENT AND SUPPLIES (32)
☐ SERVICE, TRADE, AND MAINTENANCE EQUIPMENT AND SUPPLIES (35)
☐ AGRICULTURAL MACHINERY, EQUIPMENT, SUPPLIES, ETC. (37)
☐ MATERIAL HANDLING EQUIPMENT (39)
☐ BUILDINGS' EQUIPMENT, MATERIALS, AND SUPPLIES (41)
☐ TOOLS AND HARDWARE (51)
☐ PREFABRICATED STRUCTURES (Includes Mobile Homes) (54)
☐ ELECTRICAL, ELECTRONIC, AND COMMUNICATION EQUIPMENT, COMPONENTS, SUPPLIES, ETC. (58)
☐ MEDICAL, DENTAL, VETERINARY, AND LABORATORY EQUIPMENT, INSTRUMENTS, SUPPLIES, ETC. (65)
☐ PHOTOGRAPHIC EQUIPMENT AND SUPPLIES (67)
☐ CHEMICALS, FUELS, GASES, AND OILS, RELATED PRODUCTS AND EQUIPMENT (68)
☐ DATA PROCESSING EQUIPMENT AND SUPPLIES (70)
☐ HOUSEHOLD FURNITURE, FURNISHINGS, AND APPLIANCES (72)
☐ OFFICE MACHINES, FURNITURE, FURNISHINGS, SUPPLIES AND DEVICES (74)
☐ ORES, MINERALS, AND THEIR PRIMARY PRODUCTS (96)
☐ JEWELRY, WATCHES, CLOTHING, PERSONAL ITEMS, ETC. (99)

RECYCLABLE (SCRAP AND WASTE MATERIALS)

☐ FOOD WASTE (Grease, Fat, Bones, Etc.) (01)
☐ MAGNETIC TAPES (ADP, Audio, Video) (02)
☐ PAPER (e.g., Newsprint, Manila cards) (03)
☐ PRECIOUS METALS (Includes Items/materials containing precious metals) (04)
☐ FERROUS AND NONFERROUS METALS (05)
☐ TEXTILES (Includes Leather Products and Synthetic Fabrics) (06)
☐ WASTE OILS, FUELS, LUBRICANTS, CHEMICALS (07)
☐ SALVAGE/SCRAP VEHICLES (08)
☐ OTHER WASTES (09)

☐ ALL OF THE ABOVE PERSONAL PROPERTY (CODES 10 THRU 99)

0007 Data Processing Equipment
0008 Electrical: Supplies and Equipment (Motors, Generators, Transformers)
0009 Electronic and Communications Equipment
0010 Food Preparation, Dishwashing and Serving Equipment
0011 Furniture: Office and Household
0012 Hardware and Tools
0013 Heavy Construction, Transportation and Materials Handling Equipment
0014 Laundry, Detergents and Other Cleaning Supplies
0015 Maintenance and Ship Equipment
0016 Medical, Dental and Laboratory Equipment
0017 Office Machines, Printing and Duplicating Equipment and Supplies
0018 Photographic Supplies and Equipment
0019 Plumbing Equipment, Pumps and Compressors
0020 Structures, Prefabricated
0021 Mobile Homes and House Trailers
0022 Other (Miscellaneous)
0023 Food Waste (Grease, Fat, Bones, Etc.)
0024 Scrap Metal
0025 Paper
0026 Waste Oils, Fuels, Lubricants, Chemicals
0027 Other Wastes (Leather, Textiles, Plastic, Etc.)

Once you've filled out your application, mail it back to GSA -- they'll even pay for the postage -- and soon you'll begin to receive GSA Sales Catalogs containing some of the items in which you might have an interest. (See FIGURE 13 on page 44 for an example of what GSA Sales Catalogs look like.)

4.3 GSA METHODS OF SALE

Surplus personal property is sold to the public by competitive bid using one of three sale methods. No preferences are given to individuals, veterans or religious organizations.

Sealed Bid: An "Invitations for Bids" (IFB) and bidding form are provided to the prospective buyer. The IFB describes the property offered for sale, lists special conditions applicable to the sale, and indicates where and when bids must be submitted. Sealed bids received at the specified sales office by the date and time shown in the IFB are opened publicly. Awards are made to the highest responsive bidders and the sales office notifies the successful bidders as soon as possible.

Auction: Traditional auction methods are used. Prospective buyers are given a description of the property to be auctioned and bidding instructions. The auctioneer "crying" the sale offers the property item-by-item and awards each item to the highest responsive bidder.

Spot Bid: Bidding takes place during the sale and the property is offered item by item, as in an auction. However, bids are written rather than voiced. Awards to the highest responsive bidders are announced.

4.4   GSA CONDITIONS OF SALE

General Conditions: Surplus property is sold subject to the General Sale Terms and Conditions (Standard Form 114C). COPIES ARE AVAILABLE FOR REVIEW AT THE GSA CUSTOMER SERVICE BUREAU SERVING YOUR AREA.

Special Conditions: Special restrictions and conditions often apply to the sale of certain classes of property. Bidders should study carefully their sales invitations and catalogs to be sure they understand the terms of each sale.

Awards: Property is awarded to bidders who submit the highest bids acceptable to the Government and responsive to the terms and conditions in the IFB. If none of the bids represents a fair price (equal to the market value of the property), an award might not be made, and the property would be re-offered for sale at a later date.

Payment and Removal: Successful bidders cannot remove any property they have been awarded until they have paid for it in full. Acceptable forms of payment are cash, money orders, traveler's checks, cashier's checks, PERSONAL CHECKS WITH INFORMAL BANK LETTERS GUARANTEEING PAYMENT, credit union checks, and Government checks.

4.5   GSA VEHICLE AUCTIONS

The following descriptions are taken from an article appearing in a national magazine describing a GSA auction in Washington, DC.   You'll find several tips of value to you.   This particular auction was selling cars, trucks and other vehicles.

"... one of the myths about the surplus sales is that they are the exclusive province of used-car dealers ... NOT TRUE ... 95% or so are general public; maybe 5% are dealers ....   The dealers cannot compete since they have to buy for resale; if you can get a vehicle for what they would pay, you're effectively getting it at wholesale -- at dealer's cost."

"... The stars of the show are any and all pickup trucks ....   A small fleet of 1977 imports (automobiles) were originally bought by the Department of Transportation for brake ... seat belt testing, etc. None with over 250 miles, they included a Renault Le Car, a Toyota Celica, a Honda Accord ... an Audi Fox, a BMW 320i and a Porsche 924 ....   As it happened, the testing was never done, so the cars were in fact new."

"So far, the prices paid have followed a vague pattern: Under $300 for any visibly abused vehicle; $350 to $800 for sedans more than 5 years old; $800 to $900 for stations wagons; $700 to $1400 for late model sedans (except American Motors products, which usually sell for $200 to $500 less); $500 to $1500 for pickup trucks."

"... Prices hover near wholesale.   Some are below, some above."

"... The Porsche 924 cost DOT $9250; book value is $8000.   It sold for $7250.   A good deal -- not cheap, not a gift, but definitely good."

4.6   A REVIEW

Here's what we've covered in this section about GSA surplus:

*   You've learned how GSA acquires property it sells from other Government agencies and from Drug Enforcement Administration seizures.

*   You've learned how to get on GSA's mailing list so you can receive FREE auction and sales catalogs for any of the regions in the United States.

*   We've explained GSA's "Usable Property & Supplies Equipment Code" so you'll know how to order catalogs for the specific types of property in which you're interested.

*   We've explained the three methods of sale and GSA's Terms and Conditions

*   You've learned what an incredible variety of items are sold by GSA ... and hopefully you're going to take advantage of some of the great opportunities offered by GSA as soon as you start receiving sales catalogs!

5.0   U.S. POSTAL SERVICE

The United States Postal Service is yet another interesting source for Government surplus ... in the form of jeeps and undeliverable parcels.

5.1   JEEPS

The U.S. Postal Service uses a VERY large quantity of 2-wheel drive jeeps as delivery vehicles. When these jeeps are retired from service, they are sold to the general public, sometimes at **very attractive prices**. One important consideration for you to remember is that all the jeeps have steering on the right-hand side, with controls on the left (which is legal to drive, but uncomfortable for some drivers). Postal Service jeep auctions are not held very often, but fantastic bargains have been found by those who wait. If you are very interested in jeeps, you may wish to wait for one of these auctions to come up. For information on future jeep sales in your area, write to:

> U.S. Postal Service
> Office of Fleet Management
> Room 7246
> 475 L'Enfant Plaza
> Washington, DC   20260

When you write, ask for the address of the U.S. Postal Service "Office of Fleet Management" that handles Postal Service vehicle sales in your own area. You also may be able to find out the same information by calling your local Post Office.

5.2   DEAD PARCELS, OR "THERE'S NO SUCH THING AS JUNK MAIL"

Have you ever wondered what happens to the thousands of packages that, for one reason or another, cannot be delivered to the people to whom they are addressed? Well, the Postal Service cannot store all these packages, so they sell them by auction to the general public. You never know what you might find at a Postal Service "Unclaimed Merchandise" auction -- just about anything that is small enough to be mailed! Books, watches, jewelry, kitchenware and clothes are all items that have been sold at past auctions.

Auctions of unclaimed or loose-in-the-mails items are held at least twice a year at each of the Postal Service's "Dead Parcel Branches." There are currently five regional centers across the country that hold auctions. To find out when and where sales are scheduled, write to the regional office below which serves your area. You can also write to the same address to be put on the mailing list for future sales.

Office 1:   General Manager
U.S. Postal Service
Dead Parcel Branch
Atlanta, Georgia   30304-9506

Serves: Alabama, Arkansas, Florida, Georgia, Louisiana, Mississippi, Oklahoma, Tennessee and Texas

Office 2:   General Manager
U.S. Postal Service
Dead Parcel Branch
Chicago, Illinois   60607-9506

Serves: Colorado, Illinois, Indiana, Iowa, Kansas, Michigan, Minnesota, Missouri, Nebraska, North Dakota, Ohio, South Dakota, Wisconsin, Wyoming

Office 3:   General Manager
U.S. Postal Service
Dead Parcel Branch
New York, NY   10199-9543

Serves: Connecticut, Massachusetts, Maine, New Hampshire, New Jersey (Zip 070-079, 088-089), New York, Puerto Rico, Rhode Island, Vermont, Virgin Islands

Office 4:   General Manager
U.S. Postal Service
Dead Parcel Branch
Philadelphia, PA   19104-9597

Serves: District of Columbia, Delaware, Kentucky, Maryland, New Jersey (Zip 080-087), North Carolina, Pennsylvania, South Carolina, Virginia, West Virginia

Office 5:   General Manager
U.S. Postal Service
Dead Parcel Branch
San Francisco, CA   94188-9661

Serves: Alaska, Arizona, California, Hawaii, Idaho, Montana, Nevada, New Mexico, Oregon, Utah, Washington, Guam, American Samoan Islands

FIGURE 15 on the following page is an example of a recent Post Office Auction notice, similar to what you will receive once you are on the mailing list. Some of the available items are identified, as well as conditions of the sale.

FIGURE 15
POST OFFICE AUCTION NOTICE

United States
Postal Service

February 1, 1990   **POST OFFICE AUCTION**

On February 15, 1990, a postal auction of incidental general merchandise will be held at the Postal Facility located at 228 Harrison Street, San Francisco, California. The auction will commence at 10:00 A.M.

A preview of the merchandise will be held at the same location, on February 15, 1990, from 8:00 A.M. to 10:00 A.M.

There will be a total of approximately 50 tub book lots, 30 lots of jewelry and watches, and 420 lots of miscellaneous merchandise. The minimum bid will be $20.00, unless indicated otherwise after the lot description in the Auction Catalog. There will be a minimum bid of $200.00 on all tub book lots. Payment must be by cash, cashier's check, certified check or U.S. Postal Money Order.

CUSTOMERS ARE REQUIRED TO FURNISH THEIR OWN CONTAINERS FOR REMOVAL OF MERCHANDISE FROM THE AUCTION AREA. ADVANCE COPIES OF THE CATALOG ARE AVAILABLE, THERE IS A NOMINAL FEE TO COVER PRINTING AND POSTAGE. PLEASE CONTACT ME AT THE ADDRESS SHOWN BELOW FOR FURTHER INFORMATION OR CALL (415) 550-5400.

Catalogues will be available at the auction site.

NOTICE: Please complete and furnish information requested below if you have moved, or wish to have your name removed from the postal auction mailing list.

/☐/ I have moved - My old address is: My new address is:
Name:_____   _____

Address:_____   _____

City/State:_____ZIP Code_____   _____ZIP Code_____

/☐/ Please remove my name from the postal auction mailing list:
Name:_____

Address:_____

City/State:_____ZIP Code_____

Be sure to furnish name, complete address including ZIP Code number. Return this form letter to the address below.

Sincerely,

Donna Autrey, Acting
Supt., Claims, Inquiry & Undeliverable Mail
U.S. Postal Service
San Francisco, CA 94188-9661

6.0 U.S. CUSTOMS SEIZURES

The United States Customs Service is a branch of the Department of Treasury that regulates import activities into the U.S. Among other things, the Customs Service assesses and collects customs duties, excise taxes, fees and penalties due on imported merchandise; intercepts and seizes contraband; processes persons, carriers, cargo and mail into and out of the United States; and apprehends persons engaged in fraudulent practices designed to circumvent customs and related laws.

Every year the U.S. Customs Service seizes a tremendous amount of contraband and property for which the owner is unable to pay the assessed duty, or which owners have tried to "sneak in" without paying the required duty. This property is later sold to the general public by auction.

6.1 WHAT WILL YOU FIND AT A U.S. CUSTOMS AUCTION?

If you're looking for exotic items, a U.S. Customs auction is the place for you to find them! Rather than generalize, here are some examples of recent auctions so you can see for yourself what was available:

Sale No.	86-52-1004
Date:	June 11, 1986
Location:	Miami, Florida
Property:	Boats and Airplanes

Sale No.	86-53-1005
Date:	June 24, 1986
Location:	Houston, Texas
Property:	Airplanes, Vehicles and Jewelry

Sale No.	86-23-1007
Date:	July 8, 1986
Location:	Mission, Texas
Property:	Parrots and Exotic Birds

Sale No.	87-52-119
Date:	February 18, 1987
Location:	Miami, Florida
Property:	Boats, Cars and Aircraft

Sale No.	87-20-139
Date:	February 20,1987
Location:	New Orleans, Louisiana
Property:	95' Freighter

FIGURE 16
U.S. CUSTOMS AUCTIONS

U.S. CUSTOMS SERVICE

Public Auction

Mission, Texas

Thursday - April 16, 1987 - 9:00 am

170 EXOTIC BIRDS

Yellow and Red Head Amazon Parrots - Canaries - Conures - Parakeets - Yellow Cheeks - Scarlet Macaws - Green Conures - Lilac Crowns

Sale No. 87-23-181

USDA Quarantine Center
Old Moore Field Highway 681
North of Mission, Texas

Inspection: 8:00 - 9:00 am April 16, 1987

For more information call Northrop Worldwide Aircraft Services, Inc., at (405) 357-9194.

NORTHROP
Northrop Worldwide
Aircraft Services, Inc.

This sale is conducted by
Northrop Worldwide Aircraft Services, Inc.
with all proceeds directed to the U.S. Treasury.

U.S. CUSTOMS SERVICE

Open Bid Auction

Vehicle may be inspected and bids placed from 8:00 am - 5:00 pm April 6th through 10th, 1987 at:

J & A Body and Fender
638 N. Helena
Spokane, WA

79 Pontiac Trans-Am
VIN - 2W87W9L140511

Complete Terms of Sale on Reverse

For more information concerning this sale call Northrop Worldwide Aircraft Services, Inc., U.S. Customs Service Support Division at (405) 357-9194.

Sale No. 87-30-182

NORTHROP
Northrop Worldwide
Aircraft Services, Inc.

This sale is conducted by
Northrop Worldwide Aircraft Services, Inc.
with all proceeds directed to the U.S. Treasury.

Sale No.   87-23-123
Date: March 7, 1987
Location: Loredo, Texas
Property: Cars, Gold Coins, Merchandise

Sale No.   87-27-150
Date: March 12, 1987
Location: Lawton, Oklahoma
Property: EIGHT 1970-72 Rolls Royces, Airbourne Surveillance
            Equipment, and Clothing

6.2   HOW TO PARTICIPATE IN U.S. CUSTOMS AUCTIONS

U.S. Customs sales are unique among Government property sales in that the sales are actually conducted by a private company -- Northrop Worldwide Aircraft Services, Inc. -- instead of being conducted by the Government itself (as in all other Government surplus programs). The proceeds of the sales are, however, directed to the U.S. Treasury.

While auction notices are no longer available free of charge, they are available at a nominal charge from Northrop Worldwide Aircraft Services Inc. The following subscription options are available:

OPTION 1: National. Subscription period covers one year from the time you order, which includes all states and customs districts in the U.S. Cost is $50.00.

OPTION 2: **Eastern U.S.** Subscription period covers one year from the time you order, which includes the Eastern U.S. and Puerto Rico. Cost is $25.00.

OPTION 3: **Western U.S.** Subscription period covers one year from the time you order, which includes the Western U.S. and Hawaii. Cost is $25.00.

If you are interested in ordering a subscription to Northrop's U.S. Customs auction notices, send a U.S. POSTAL MONEY ORDER (no other form of payment accepted) in the amount for each option with your name, full address, phone number and option number to:

Northrop Worldwide Aircraft Services Inc.
U.S. Custom Support Division
P.O. Box 2065
Lawton, OK 73502-2065

FIGURE 17 below is an example of just one U.S. Customs auction notice; jewelry, aircraft, vessels, vehicles -- exciting and exotic -- and quite typical!

FIGURE 17
U.S. CUSTOMS AUCTION NOTICE

MIAMI'S SPARKLING SPECIAL

U.S. CUSTOMS SERVICE
Public Auction

JEWELRY

**Dupont Plaza Hotel - Ballroom
300 Biscayne Boulevard Way
Miami, FL**

March 30 - Registration & Viewing: 3 pm - 6 pm. Auction: 6 pm.
March 31 - Registration & Viewing: 8 am-10am. Auction: 10 am.

VESSELS AIRCRAFT VEHICLES GENERAL PROPERTY

**Miami Port Authority
Passenger Terminal Nos. 8 & 9
Dodge Island, Miami, FL**

April 1 - Registration: 8 am. Auction: 10 am.
March 31 - Preregistration: 1 pm - 4 pm.

NORTHROP
Northrop Worldwide
Aircraft Services, Inc.

This sale is conducted by
Northrop Worldwide Aircraft Services, Inc.
with all proceeds directed to the U. S. Treasury.

7.0   INTERNAL REVENUE SERVICE AUCTIONS

The Internal Revenue Service, a division of the Department of Treasury, is yet another good Government source for seized property.   The IRS sells a wide variety of property (homes, real estate, boats, automobiles, airplanes, etc.) which have been seized from individuals and businesses due to non-payment of taxes.   If you're interested in receiving FREE notices of IRS auctions, call your local IRS office (look for "Internal Revenue Service" under U.S. Government Offices in your local phone book), and ask how you can get on the "Bidders List" for IRS auctions in your area.   Your local IRS office will give you the address you need to request auction notices for your area.   Be sure to specify what types of items you're interested in.

8.0   SMALL BUSINESS ADMINISTRATION   LIQUIDATIONS

The Small Business Administration ("SBA") is an agency of the Government whose main purpose is to help small businesses.   The SBA offers several types of financial assistance to small business owners, including **direct loans** and **guaranteed loans.**   When one of these businesses is unable to meet its loan obligations, the SBA forecloses on the loans and sells any property owned by the business to recover the money outstanding on the loan.

Because SBA is involved in helping so many types of small businesses, it's impossible to guess exactly what you'll find at an SBA liquidation sale.   Office equipment, computers, high technology equipment, restaurant equipment and agricultural equipment are just a few of the items you can expect to find at various sales.   If you're interested in business equipment, SBA liquidations are an excellent place to look.

To find out exactly what is available in your area, you'll want to contact the **Liquidations Officer** of the SBA Office which serves your area.   (The offices are listed in Appendix 3 on page 103 of this directory.)

9.0   THE ODD AND UNUSUAL: LIGHTHOUSES OR WILD HORSES, ANYONE?

The Government really can provide just about anything imaginable -- plus a few things you'd probably never dream of finding at a Government sale. How about buying a lighthouse from the Government ... or adopting wild horses and burros? Whether you need a large ship or a small load of firewood, the Government sells it! These are just a few of the unusual items we've come across in our research. The more you become involved in these sales, the more exotic discoveries you'll make! In the meantime, here are a few of the more unusual items we've found.

9.1   SO YOU'D LIKE TO ADOPT A WILD HORSE ... OR BURRO?

Believe it or not, the U.S. Government will let you adopt a wild horse or burro through the Bureau of Land Management's "Adopt-A-Horse" program. These animals are excess <u>wild</u> horses and burros that roam public lands in the western states. They are not accustomed to people, but with kindness, patience, and gentleness they can be tamed and trained just as their domestic counterparts. A typical horse stands 14 hands (or 56 inches at its shoulder) and weighs about 900 pounds. For the most part, the horses are solid colors, usually shades of brown or gray. Burros available for adopting average between 42 and 48 inches in height and weigh about 500 pounds.

Adoption fees for these animals are VERY LOW: **$125 per horse** or **$75 per burro**. No adoption fee is charged for unweaned foals accompanying their mare or jenny. Orphan foals under the age of 6 months are available infrequently and are also adopted at no fee.

You are responsible for the cost of transporting the animal to your home from the adoption center, and all costs involved in its future upkeep. Every excess wild horse or burro offered for adoption has been examined to ensure its soundness and good health. Any necessary medical treatment has been administered, so you can be sure you're getting an animal in good health.

Since 1973 more than 65,000 animals have been placed in foster home across America. It isn't difficult to qualify to adopt ... basically, the Government just wants to make sure that the animal will be well treated and will have good living conditions. To request an application form and other information relevant to this program, write to the BLM address shown below which serves your area. Besides the application, you should request the FREE booklet, "So You'd Like to Adopt a Wild Horse ... or Burro?" See

FIGURE 18 on pages 64 and 65 for an example of the application form for the Adopt-A-Horse program; and FIGURE 19 on page 66 for an example of the real thing!

U.S. DEPT OF THE INTERIOR
BUREAU OF LAND MANAGEMENT OFFICES

Bureau of Land Management
701 "C" Street
Box 13
Anchorage, AK   99513
(907) 271-5069
Area Served: Alaska

Bureau of Land Management
2015 W. Deer Valley Road
Phoenix, AZ   85027
602) 863-4463
Area Served: Arizona

Bureau of Land Management
Federal Building
2800 Cottage Way, Rm E-2841
Sacramento, CA   95825
(916) 978-4725
Area Served: California

Bureau of Land Management
2850 Youngfield
Lakewood, CO   80215
(303) 236-1748
Area Served: Colorado

Bureau of Land Management
350 South Pickett Street
Alexandria, VA   22304
(703) 274-0231
Area Served: States East of the
Mississippi River, plus Iowa, Minnesota,
Missouri, Arkansas and Louisiana

Bureau of Land Management
3380 Americana Terrace
Boise, ID   83706
(208) 334-1425
Area Served: Idaho

Bureau of Land Management
222 North 32nd Street
P.O. Box 36800
Billings, MT   59107
(406) 657-6656
Area Served: Montana, North Dakota
and South Dakota

Bureau of Land Management
Palomino Valley Wild Horse
 and Burro Adoption Center
P.O. Box 3270
Sparks, NV   89432
(702) 673-1150
Area Served: Nevada

Bureau of Land Management
Joseph M. Montoya Federal Bldg
South Federal Place
P.O. Box 1449
Santa Fe, NM   87501-1449
(505) 988-6231
Area Served: New Mexico, Kansas,
Oklahoma and Texas

Bureau of Land Management
Burns District Office
74 South Alvord Street
Burns, OR   97720
(503) 573-5241
Area Served: Oregon and Washington

Bureau of Land Management
324 South State Street
Salt Lake City, UT   84111-2303
(801) 524-3119
Area Served: Utah

Bureau of Land Management
2515 Warren Avenue
P.O. Box 1828
Cheyenne, WY   82003
(307) 772-2078
Area Served: Wyoming and Nebraska

FIGURE 18
WILD HORSE/BURRO ADOPTION APPLICATION

Form 4710-10
(November 1985)

**UNITED STATES
DEPARTMENT OF THE INTERIOR
BUREAU OF LAND MANAGEMENT**

FORM APPROVED
OMB NO. 1004-0042
Expires: January 31, 1988

APPLICATION FOR ADOPTION OF WILD HORSE(S) OR BURRO(S)

APPLICANT'S LAST NAME   FIRST   M.I.

STREET ADDRESS OR P.O. BOX

CITY   STATE   ZIP CODE

DRIVER'S LICENSE NO.   STATE   BIRTH DATE

HOME PHONE *(include area code)*   BUSINESS PHONE *(include area code)*   Mo   Day   Yr

Number of animals requested for adoption: Horses ☐☐☐   Burros ☐☐☐

Please answer the following questions:

1. Have you read and do you understand the PROHIBITED ACTS and the TERMS OF ADOPTION on the reverse side? ☐ Yes ☐ No

2. Describe the facilities that will be provided to the animals you have requested.

   a. Shelter size, height, and construction materials:

   b. Corral size, fence height and construction materials:

   c. Pasture size:

   d. Feed and water:

3. Will more than four untitled wild horses or burros be kept at the location where you will keep the animals requested in this application? ☐ Yes ☐ No

4. Will someone other than you select, transport, or care for the animals requested? ☐ Yes ☐ No

5. Have you previously adopted animals through the Federal Government's Wild Horse and Burro Adoption Program? ☐ Yes ☐ No

6. Have you ever been convicted of abuse or inhumane treatment of animals, violation of the Wild Free Roaming Horse and Burro Act or the Wild Horse and Burro Regulations? ☐ Yes ☐ No

_____   _____
(Signature of Applicant)   (Date)

Title 18 U.S.C. Section 1001, makes it a crime for any person knowingly and willfully to make to any department or agency of the United States any false, fictitious, or fraudulent statements or representation as to any matter within its jurisdiction.

INSTRUCTIONS

1. Carefully read the PROHIBITED ACTS and TERMS OF ADOPTION printed below.

2. Carefully read the information provided in the pamphlet *"So You'd Like to Adopt a Wild Horse... or Burro?"*

3. Submit your completed Application for Adoption of Wild Horse(s) or Burro(s) to the BLM office serving your State. (For the correct address, refer to the pamphlet *"So You'd Like to Adopt a Wild Horse... or Burro?"*)

4. So that we may notify you when and where the animal(s) you requested are available, provide the Bureau of Land Management office serving your State within 10 days of any change in your address or telephone number.

TERMS OF ADOPTION

The following terms apply to all wild horses and burros adopted under this Private Care and Maintenance Agreement:

(a) Adopters are financially responsible for providing proper care;

(b) Adopters are responsible, as provided by State law, for any personal injury, property damage, or death caused by animals in their care, for pursuing animals that escape or stray, and for costs of recapture;

(c) Adopters shall not transfer animals for more than 30 days to another location or to the care of another individual without the prior approval of the authorized officer;

(d) Adopters shall make animals available for physical inspection within 7 days of receipt of a written request by the authorized officer;

(e) Adopters shall notify the authorized officer within 7 days of discovery of an animal's death, theft or escape;

(f) Adopters shall notify the authorized officer within 30 days of any change in the adopter's address;

(g) Adopters shall dispose of remains in accordance with applicable sanitation laws; and

(h) Title shall remain with the Federal Government for at least 1 year after the Private Maintenance and Care Agreement is executed and until a Certificate of Title is issued by the authorized officer.

Failure to comply with these terms may result in the cancellation of the agreement, repossession of the animals, and disapproval of requests for adoption of additional animals. In addition, violation of any term of a Private Maintenance and Care Agreement is a prohibited act. Any person who commits a prohibited act shall be subject to a fine of not more than $2,000 or imprisonment for not more than one year, or both, for each violation.

PROHIBITED ACTS

(a) Maliciously or negligently injuring or harassing a wild horse or burro;

(b) Removing or attempting to remove a wild horse or burro from the public lands without authorization from the authorized officer;

(c) Destroying a wild horse or burro without authorization from the authorized officer, except as an act of mercy;

(d) Selling or attempting to sell a wild horse or burro or its remains;

(e) Treating a wild horse or burro inhumanely;

(f) Commercially exploiting a wild horse or burro;

(g) Branding a wild horse or burro;

(h) Removing or altering a freeze mark on a wild horse or burro;

(i) Violating an order, term, or condition established by the authorized officer under this part.

Any person who commits a prohibited act shall be subject to a fine of not more than $2,000 or imprisonment for not more than one year, or both, for each violation.

NOTICE

The Privacy Act of 1974 and the regulation in 43 CFR 2.48(d) provide that you be furnished the following information in connection with information required by this agreement.

AUTHORITY: 16 U.S.C. 1333

PRINCIPAL PURPOSE: The information is to be used to process your agreement for private maintenance of wild horses or burros.

ROUTINE USES: (1) Documentation of public information. (2) Information from the record and/or the record will be transferred to appropriate Federal, State, or local agencies, when relevant to civil, criminal, or regulatory investigations or prosecutions.

EFFECT OF NOT PROVIDING INFORMATION: Disclosure of the information is voluntary. If all the information is not provided, your application cannot be processed.*

The Paperwork Reduction Act of 1980 (44 U.S.C. 3501, et seq.) requires us to inform you that:

This information is being collected to process your application to adopt a wild horse or burro.

This information will be used to determine your qualifications to provide proper care to a wild horse or burro.

Response to this request is voluntary.

*NOTE: If your driver's license and Social Security number are identical, disclosure of the driver's license number is voluntary. Failure to disclose your license number in this case will not result in the disapproval of this Agreement.

FIGURE 19
WILD HORSES AND BURROS

9.2 SURPLUS FEDERAL REAL ESTATE -- WOULD YOU LIKE TO BUY A LIGHTHOUSE?

Yes, once in awhile the Federal Government sells some really unusual real estate: lighthouses, beachfront property in Hawaii, etc., and sometimes (not always) at rock-bottom prices. Take a look at the newspaper articles we've reproduced in FIGURE 20 on page 68, entitled "SURPLUS OREGON LIGHTHOUSE COULD MAKE OWNER A MILLIONAIRE!" This story tells how an Oregon man bought a lighthouse from the Government for just $27,000 -- **which he later offered for sale for $750,000.00!** We don't know if he had any takers at that price but obviously he got a good deal from the Government.

Lighthouses are not always available; however, the Federal Government always has several interesting surplus properties for sale. To receive a FREE LIST of upcoming sales of Surplus Federal Real estate every month, write to:

> S. James
> Consumer Information Center-A
> P.O. Box 100
> Pueblo, CO 81002

Request the booklet entitled "Sales of Federal Surplus Real Estate," Item #567R. **NO MAILING LIST IS MAINTAINED, so be sure to reorder each month.**

The Consumer Information Center (a branch of the General Services Administration) distributes a wide variety of FREE and LOW COST information booklets about Government programs. You might also want to request a FREE copy of its quarterly entitled "Consumer Information Catalog."

In addition to ordering this free list, it's a good idea to watch for surplus real estate sales in the Government's daily newspaper, COMMERCE BUSINESS DAILY, which is available in most public libraries.

Good luck -- and let us know if YOU buy a lighthouse!

FIGURE 20
NEWSPAPER ARTICLES

Govt. Sells Billions of Dollars Worth of Goods Belonging to Taxpayers at a Fraction of Their Original Cost

If someone came into your home and forced you to sell your $500 color TV set for $35, what would your reaction be?

You'd protest — rightfully — that you were being robbed.

But that is exactly what's happening to you in Washington, where two government agencies regularly sell billions of dollars' worth of goods belonging to you, the taxpayer, at a fraction of their original cost.

The average rate of return on most government surplus items is shockingly low — a mere 7 cents on the dollar.

But many of the surplus items that are sold by the General Services Administration (GSA) and the Dept. of Defense return even less to the public treasury.

For example, 112 helicopters that cost the taxpayers $9.2 million were declared surplus by the Army and were sold for only $157,000 — a return of less than 2 cents on the dollar.

What does "surplus" mean? Not necessarily useless, broken down or even damaged — just goods not wanted any more.

Late model cars, for instance, with thousands of good miles left in them, regularly go on the auction block simply because some government agency wants newer models. GSA is lucky if it gets a few hundred dollars for them.

Another example: An 82-acre former missile installation in my home state of Idaho, which cost the Air Force $33 million to buy and build, was sold to the highest bidder for only $5,500. Where else could you get land for $67 an acre?

These aren't sales — they're robberies. And the taxpayers were the ones who got robbed.

The way the items are put on sale almost guarantees a low return. Announcements of the sales are sent to 25,000 names on the Dept. of Defense's mailing list — mostly dealers with inside knowledge.

Most citizens don't know the sales are taking place. If they did they could buy a used lawn mower, typewriter or car at these discounts.

Tax-weary Americans should demand their throwaway-minded government officials adopt a new motto.

"Use it up, wear it out, make it do — or do without!"

Surplus Oregon Lighthouse Could Make Owner A Millionaire!

Can you still make money buying Government Surplus Properties? You bet - For example - Max Shillock, Jr., says he isn't really interested in selling the Tillamook, Oregon Lighthouse - but an offer in the neighborhood of $750,000 to $1 million might change his mind.

Shillock, 27, bought the surplus lighthouse last February for $27,000. Recently an ad appeared in The Los Angeles Times offering the 1½ acre rock and the three-story lighthouse for sale at $750,000.

Shillock said the Los Angeles realty firm of Shields & Styne approached him about selling the historic property, but he intends to keep the lighthouse.

"Of course, if someone were to offer me $1 million for it, or even $750,000, I would have to take a look at the offer. That's the American Way."

Gary Woods, one of two agents at Shields & Styne trying to find "a big-moneyed buyer" for the vintage-1880 lighthouse, says he doesn't think the asking price will scare away potential buyers. "It will sell out of the blue to someone who really is looking for something different and who has the money."

Shillock, meanwhile, is looking for a helicopter pilot who will ferry him to the lighthouse off the North Oregon coast on a regular basis for a reduced price.

You Can Get REAL Bargains at U.S. Customs Service Auctions
...Like a $75,000 Plane Engine for $500

In the market for a few bales of tobacco? A dinosaur bone? A case of English pickled onions? A coffin? One hundred manhole covers?

You may find just what you're looking for at a U.S. Customs Service auction.

"You can get a lot of bargains at these auctions," says Alfred Balasbas, a supervisory customs inspector for the Honolulu District Customs Office.

"One ring worth about $35,000 was auctioned off for about $8,000. A prefabricated mahogany house without blueprints worth about $25,000 went for around $4,500.

"We have had airplane engines worth as much as $75,000 sell for $500," he said.

Customs auctions are held in 45 American cities at various times and they are usually advertised in newspapers. Items sold have been abandoned, detained, unclaimed or seized from smugglers. Last year, the auctions brought in revenues of $2,887,354.

And some of the sales items are real lulus.

"We sold a dinosaur bone for $50 and a casket for $150," said Jerome Hollander, public affairs officer for U.S. Customs, Los Angeles Region.

"We have also sold three belly dancer costumes, a horse-drawn cart from Ireland, two new sailing yachts, a 1942 bus, 200 cases of bras, a case of cricket bats and balls, 5 cases of beards and mustaches, and 3 bulletproof sports coats."

You may get some real buys, said Dennis Orphan, regional public affairs officer for U.S. Customs in San Francisco.

"One fellow bought a carton of VW parts worth about $2,000 for $700. Another guy paid $600 for a Mercedes-Benz with no engine; another bought a $9,000 solar collection unit for home heating for $3,500."

Martin Bond, inspector with the U.S. Customs at Norfolk, Va., told The ENQUIRER:

"Items sold at a recent auction included three automobile tire rims for $17; seven bales of tobacco for $35, and a wall tapestry for $15."

Other items sold include a case of left-footed shoes, 4 bales of ¼ by 12 inch rubber strips, a coffin, Italian furniture, 162 boxes containing an assortment of rocks, 25 cases of insect repellent, 6 unassembled modern plastic school desks, boxes of underwear, and 120 cartons of bingo sheets, according to Jim Dingfelder, public affairs officer for U.S. Customs, Miami Region.

Harriet Harris, former secretary to the district director of Customs for Portland, Oreg., district, added: "We have sold 3 cartons of bulldozer track pins, a sack of Guatemalan coffee, a case of English pickled onions, 138 dozen straw hats and 100 manhole covers."

Customs auctions are held on an irregular basis in 45 cities across the U.S. In larger cities, they may be held monthly, while in smaller cities, auctions may be held only once a year.

You can find out what cities hold Customs auctions by writing to: U.S. Customs Service, Office of Information, 1301 Constitution Ave. N.W., Washington, D.C. 20229. For dates of auctions, you must contact the individual Customs office.

ARE YOU IN the market for a used car? An aircraft? Plumbing and heating equipment?

Or perhaps you're looking for a good buy in a typewriter or an office machine for your business? Medical items, textiles, hardware, furniture?

The U.S. government may have a good buy for you. A wide variety of personal property throughout the nation is continuously being offered for sale by the federal government, with the General Services Administration and the Department of Defense the principal government agencies engaged in selling personal property.

But sales of civil agency personal property are regularly conducted by the GSA, the giant purchasing arm of the federal government — including a long list of consumer-type items. Each of the ten GSA regional offices conducts sales and each office maintains a mailing list for the geographical area it serves.

You can obtain a mailing list application to have your name placed on the GSA mailing list by writing to the GSA, Federal Supply Service, Personal Property Department in the regional area serving your locality. (See your phone book under U.S. Government.)

9.3   FREE FIREWOOD FROM THE FOREST SERVICE

A program of the U.S. Department of Agriculture's Forest Service makes firewood available from 155 National Forests. Depending upon the supply and demand, free firewood may occasionally be obtained from some forests. Usually, there is a minimum $10 charge for the wood -- still a great bargain!

Before cutting wood in any National Forest, a permit must be obtained from the District Ranger. The District Ranger will also provide information on where to cut wood, how much wood can be removed, and whether or not free wood is available. District Ranger offices are listed in the telephone directory under U.S. Government, Agriculture Department, Forest Service. If none is listed, contact the office closest to your area from the following list and ask for the address and phone number of the District Ranger closest to your area.

REGIONAL HEADQUARTERS OF THE FOREST SERVICE

U.S. Forest Service
Federal Building
P.O. Box 7669
Missoula, MT
Area Served: Idaho and Montana

U.S. Forest Service
Federal Building
517 Gold Avenue, SW
Albuquerque, NM   87102
Area Served: Arizona and New Mexico

U.S. Forest Service
630 Sansome Street
San Francisco, CA   94111
Area Served: California

U.S. Forest Service
11177 West 8th Street
P.O. Box 25127
Lakewood, CO   80225
Area Served: Colorado, Nebraska, South Dakota and Wyoming (Gibhorn, Medicine Bow and Shoshone)

U.S. Forest Service
324 25th Street
Ogden, UT   84401
Area Served: Idaho, Nevada, Utah and Wyoming (Bridger-Teton)

U.S. Forest Service
319 S.W. Pine Street
P.O. Box 3623
Portland, OR   97208
Area Served: Oregon and Washington

U.S. Forest Service
310 W. Wisconsin Avenue
Milwaukee, WI   53203
Area Served: Illinois, Indiana, Ohio, Michigan, Minnesota, Missouri, New Hampshire, Maine, Pennsylvania, Vermont, West Virginia and Wisconsin

U.S. Forest Service
1720 Peachtree Road NW
Atlanta, GA   30367
Area Served: Alabama, Arkansas, Florida, Georgia, Kentucky, Louisiana, Mississippi, North Carolina, Puerto Rico, South Carolina, Tennessee, Texas and Virginia

U.S. Forest Service
Federal Office Building
P.O. Box 1628
Juneau, AK   99802
Area Served: Alaska

9.4   SALES LISTS FOR U.S. REAL PROPERTY

Every quarter the Federal Property Resources Service (FPRS) of the U.S. General Services Administration publishes a list of U.S. Real Property that is for sale. FPRS has offices throughout the U.S. and is one of the nation's largest real estate sales organizations. Hundreds of millions of dollars worth or property is sold each and every year, with the proceeds going to our government.

The FPRS Real Property Sales program handles real property in all 50 states -- PLUS Puerto Rico, the U.S. Virgin Islands, and the U.S. Pacific territories. The types and values of properties sold have a range that is so varied, there is usually something available for just about any budget or need. You can find everything from former Federal office buildings, small parcels of unimproved land, high-rise building sites in large cities, industrial development acreage, warehouses, estate on the waterfront, individual residences, and military family housing. As you can see, the list is inclusive of just about every type of property!

Excess Federal real estate is usually offered first for direct transfer to other Federal agencies and then for sale or discount transfer to state and local governments or tax-supported agencies. Lands and buildings that are not transferred in this way are then offered for sale to the general public by competitive bid.

Properties may be sold by sealed bid, whereby prospective buyers submit their bids on a special bidding form. These bids are opened on a specified date, and the property is awarded to the highest bidder. The most common way for these properties to be sold is at an auction. The law requires that all properties be sold at fair market value.

The quarterly U.S. Real Property Sales List gives people interested in buying the most up-to-date information available about these properties. To keep things simple, the list divides the U.S. into four regions in which sales properties are then listed by state and city or county. The list also includes a map for each region with markers showing approximately where each property is located. Telephone numbers are provided for each region so that you can gather more information. A brief description of the property, how it will be sold, and when the sales date is scheduled is also included with the list.

When U.S. Government real property is being offered for sale, a local General Services Administration (GSA) real estate office prepares a notice that briefly describes the property and explains how, when and where it will be sold. Notices are mailed to individuals who have indicated an interest in properties of this type, value and location. How do you let them know you are interested? You can send a postcard to:

PROPERTIES
Consumer Information Center
Pueblo, CO 81009

Tell them your name, street address, apartment number (if applicable), city, and state, plus zip. They will send you their current quarterly listing.

If you want to know about individual sales you can contact:

U.S. General Services Administration
525 Market Street
San Francisco, CA 94105

Tell them the type of property you are interested in (i.e., agricultural, timber, grazing and minerals; industrial and commercial; buildings and other improvements for off-site use; or residential and waterfront resort). You will also need to let them know how high a value you are looking for in a property. They have property valued as follows: Under $100,000; $100,000 to $300,000; $300,000 to $1 million; and $1 million or more.

The GSA has designated four-digit numbers to indicate various states and territories. They are coded as follows:

0001 - AL	0019 - IA	0033 - NH	0048 - TX
0002 - AK	0020 - KS	0034 - NJ	0049 - UT
0004 - AZ	0021 - KY	0035 - NM	0050 - VT
0005 - AR	0022 - LA	0036 - NY	0051 - VA
0006 - CA	0023 - ME	0037 - NC	0053 - WA
0008 - CO	0024 - MD	0038 - ND	0054 - WV
0009 - CT	0025 - MA	0039 - OH	0055 - WI
0010 - DE	0026 - MI	0040 - OK	0056 - WV
0012 - FL	0027 - MN	0041 - OR	0057 - Am. Samoa
0013 - GA	0028 - MS	0042 - PA	0011 - DC
0015 - HI	0029 - MO	0044 - RI	0058 - Guam
0016 - ID	0030 - MT	0045 - SC	0043 - PR
0017 - IL	0031 - NE	0046 - SD	0059 - Pac.Is.Terr.
0018 - IN	0032 - NV	0047 - TN	0052 - VI

You can indicate as many as three (3) different locations. So if you are interested in properties in Indiana, Michigan and Missouri, you would tell them that you would like information on 0018; 0026; and 0029.

If you want information on all types and values of real property all over the 50 states, territories, etc., simply indicate that you are interested in **All Locations, Types, and Values.** You will then be sent information notices from all of the GSA's local real estate offices. You should also send them your daytime phone number, so that the GSA can call you about special sales or changes in sale conditions.

Remember, the GSA <u>does not</u> keep a list of names for future issues of the U.S. Real Property Sales List, so you will need to contact them every quarter to obtain their current list.

10.0 OTHER SOURCES OF GOVERNMENT SURPLUS

So far we've covered the major FEDERAL Government sources of surplus and seized property, but you should also be aware that government agencies at the **State, City and County levels** also frequently sell used office equipment, furniture and real estate, as well as lots and abandoned items such as cars and bicycles.

Many of these sales are advertised in local newspapers, on radio and television. Keep your eyes and ears open for these announcements .... better yet, open your phone book to the section of State, City and County Government offices. Start calling different agencies to find out when and where they hold their surplus property auctions; the Police Department is a great place to start. They often pick up stolen goods or people turn in things they have found; when no owner is ever found for these items, they are sold with a periodic Police Department Sale.

Don't get discouraged if the first person who answers your first call can't help you ... it's not at all unusual to be transferred from one office to another before you get the right answer to your questions. Be ready with questions to ask (write them down before you call!), and have paper and pen ready (together with your most friendly "telephone voice") when you're asking for information. You'll very likely find that most government employees are very courteous and will go out of their way to be helpful; just remember to be patient, polite, and persevere! If the first person you talk to doesn't know the answer to your question, don't give up; ask if they can refer you to someone who might be able to help you.

Here are just a few ideas you may wish to use for your local area:

Who to Call ...	And Ask About:
City Hall	City-owned real estate for sale Office equipment auctions
Fire Department	Vehicle auctions
Library	Book sales
Public Works Department	Truck and Equipment auctions
Police Department	Vehicle and abandoned property auctions
Sheriff's Department	Vehicle and abandoned property auctions
County General Services	Office equipment, furniture and vehicle auctions

Parks Department	Vehicle and maintenance equipment auctions
Transportation Department	Trucks and equipment auctions
State Lands Division	State-owned real estate for sale
State Finance Department, or State Escheaters Office	Abandoned property sales

Although State, City and County sales are of a smaller magnitude than Federal Surplus Sales, nevertheless these sales do provide a great deal of valuable property to those who take advantage of them. Don't neglect this little-used surplus market -- you may be pleasantly surprised at what you can buy without even leaving town!

11.0 CONCLUSION

Well, it's pretty exciting, isn't it? I know you're surprised to find out what an incredible assortment of items are available from the U.S. Government. The Federal Government owns a tremendous amount of real property, equipment and vehicles ... much of which is regularly sold to the general public when it is no longer useful to the Government.

According to the most recent estimate, the Federal Government owns over 460,000 motor vehicles which cost it in excess of one trillion dollars ($1,000,000,000). Of the 460,000 vehicles, roughly 183,000 are used by civilian agencies, 132,000 by the U.S. Postal Service, and 144,000 by the Department of Defense. Of the aggregate 460,000 vehicles, there are approximately 100,000 sedans, 16,000 station wagons, 329,000 trucks and 14,000 buses. Every year the Government sells over 25,000 of these vehicles to the general public .... that's over 2,000 vehicles per month!

As you've discovered by reading this directory, you can find just about anything you want at a Government sale **if you know how to look.** Using the information we've given you, you now know how to buy cars, trucks, office equipment, houses, land, aircraft, boats, computers, furniture, laboratory equipment, paints, ships, tools, tractors, live animals, luxury cars, firewood and hundreds of other valuable surplus or seized items.

To give you some more ideas of what kinds of opportunities others have found in Government sales, we've included copies of some of our favorite "surplus success stories" clipped from newspapers across the country. These articles are shown in FIGURE 20 (page 68); read them, and you'll get even more excited about the great surplus bargains .... and the next thing you know, you'll be creating your own surplus success story! Then take a look at Appendix 2 on page 93 to see where some past sales have been held. You'll very likely find several in your own general area.

So now that you're convinced that you can find fantastic bargains at Government surplus sales, here's what you must do:

STEP ONE:

Write to DoD for your **Surplus Property Bidders Application Form** (use Card #1 enclosed).

STEP TWO:

Write to GSA for your **Surplus Personal Property Mailing List Application** (use Card #2 also enclosed).

STEP THREE:

Look into other potential sources of surplus property, for example: U.S. Customs (page 57), IRS auctions (page 60), SBA Liquidations (page 60).

STEP FOUR:

Start attending auctions. Before you know it, **YOU'LL BE AN EXPERT AT FINDING FANTASTIC BARGAINS!**

Good luck in your search!

APPENDICES

APPENDIX 1

CLASSES OF SURPLUS PERSONAL PROPERTY
SOLD BY THE DEPARTMENT OF DEFENSE

Class	Description
	Recyclable Materials
8305A	Textiles including Synthetic Fabric
9450A	Paper (e.g. newsprint, manila cards)
9450B	Rubber (e.g., tires and tubes
9450C	Miscellaneous (e.g. leather, plastic, fiberglass, etc.)
9450D	Exposed Film/Spent Hypo Solution
9450E	Waste Oil, Jet Fuels, Paints, Chemicals, Waxes and Lubricants
9450F	Food Waste
9450E	Industrial Diamond Containing Materials
9660A	Precious Metals, All Types
9660B	Gold and Silver Plated or Brazed on Base Metal
9660C	Cast Iron
9670D	Prepared Heavy Melting Steel
9670E	Unprepared Heavy Melting Steel
9670F	Prepared Light Steel (black and/or galvanized)
9670G	Unprepared Light Steel (black and/or galvanized)
9670H	Unprepared Mixed Heavy and Light Steel
9670J	Turnings and Borings (steel and/or wrought iron)
9670K	Stainless Steel Alloys, Magnetic and Nonmagnetic (e.g., 300 and 400 series types except types 3190 and 446 of the American Iron and Steel Institute)
9670L	High Temperature Alloys: Nickel and Cobalt Base which are Copper Free
9680B	Copper, Copper-Base Alloys and Copper Containing Materials
9680C	Copper-Bearing Materials (e.g., motors, armatures, generators, etc. but excludes electrical and electronic materials
9680D	Miscellaneous Electrical and Electronic Materials (includes steel or aluminum armored cable, etc. but excludes copper-bearing materials)
9680E	Aluminum and aluminum Alloys (excludes material in Class 9680F)
9680F	Aircraft sold for recovery of basic metal content, parts and components
9680G	Magnesium Alloys
9680H	Lead, Lead-Base Alloys, Antimony, Zinc and Zinc Alloys (includes lead-acid type storage batteries)
9680J	Bullet and Projectile Metals (to be recovered from target, artillery and bombing ranges)
9680K	Storage Batteries (nickel-iron-alkaline types)
9680L	Storage Batteries (silver-zinc, nickel-cadmium and mercury types)
9680M	Tin and Alloys (includes tin-base babitt metal and block tin pipe, but excludes tin cans and terneplate)

USABLE PROPERTY

Weapons (Accessories)

1005   Holsters, slings, small arms accessories

Nuclear Ordnance Equipment

1190   Specialized Test and Handling Equipment, Nuclear Ordnance (e.g. specially designed trucks and trailers,slings and hoists, etc.)

Fire Control Equipment

1220   Fire Control Computing Sights and Devices
1240   Optical Sighting and Ranging Equipment
1260   Fire Control Designating and Indicating Equipment
1265   Fire Control Transmitting and Receiving Equipment, except Airborne
1270   Aircraft Gunnery Fire Control Components
1280   Aircraft Bombing Fire Control Components
1285   Fire Control Radar Equipment, except Airborne
1290   Miscellaneous Fire Control Equipment (e.g., Control Directors and Systems, Stabilizing Mechanisms, and Sonar Equipment)

Guided Missile Equipment

1440   Launchers, Guided Missile
1450   Guided Missile Handling and Servicing Equipment (e.g., specially designed trucks and trailers, slings, hoists, jacks, etc.)

Aircraft; and Airframe Structural Components

1510A   Single Engine Aircraft
1510B   Twin Engine Aircraft
1510C   Multi-Engine Aircraft
1520   Aircraft, Rotary Wing (e.g., helicopters)
1550   Drones (e.g., complete drones used for targets, training, surveillance, etc.)
1560A   Airframe Structural Components, etc., peculiar to Single Engine Aircraft
1560B   Airframe Structural Components, etc., peculiar to Multi-Engine Aircraft
1560C   Airframe Structural Components, etc., peculiar to Helicopters

Aircraft Components and Accessories

1610   Aircraft Propellers and Component Parts
1615   Helicopter Rotor Blades, Drive Mechanisms and Components (e.g., rotors,yokes, blades, blade sets, clutches, transmissions, etc.)
1620   Aircraft Landing Gear Components
1630   Aircraft Wheel and Brake Systems
1650   Aircraft Hydraulic, Vacuum, and Deicing System Components
1660   Aircraft Air Conditioning, Heating and Pressurizing Equipment

1670	Parachutes and Aerial Pick Up, Delivery, and Cargo Tie Down Equipment
1680	Miscellaneous Aircraft Accessories and Components

Aircraft Launching, Landing and Ground Handling Equipment

1710	Aircraft Arresting, Barrier, and Barricade Equipment
1720	Aircraft Launching Equipment
1730	Aircraft and Space Vehicle Ground Handling and Servicing Equipment
1740	Airfield Specialized Trucks and Trailers

Ships, Small Craft, Pontoons, and Floating Docks

1905A	Aircraft Carriers (for scrapping only)
1905B	Battleships, Cruisers, Destroyers (for scrapping only)
1905C	Landing Ships (e.g., LSM, LSMR, LSSL, LST, etc.)
1905D	Minehunters, Minesweepers, Minelayers
1905E	Submarines (for scrapping only)
1905F	Landing Craft (e.g., LCVP, LCPL, LCM, etc.)
1910	Transport Vessels, Passenger and Troop
1915	Cargo and Tanker Vessels
1925A	Ferry
1925B	Harbor Utility Craft
1925C	Repair Ships
1925D	Tugs (e.g., YTV, YTL, ATA, etc.)
1930A	Fuel Barge, Gasoline Barge, Water Barge
1930B	Lighters (open and covered)
1935	Barges and Lighters, Special Purpose (e.g., derrick piledriver, torpedo testing barges, barge-mounted cranes, etc.)
1940B	Patrol Craft (e.g., PC, PCS, SC, YP, PCE, etc.)
1940C	Seaplane Tenders
1940D	Small Craft under 40 feet in length powered and non-powered
1945	Pontoons an floating Docks (e.g., pontoon ramps, etc.
1950	Floating Docks
1990	Miscellaneous (all other vessels and service craft not included in property category numbers 1905A through 1950)

Ship and Marine Equipment

2010	Ship and Boat Propulsion Components (excludes engines and turbines
2020	Rigging and Rigging Gear
2030	Deck Machinery
2040	Marine Hardware and Hull Items (e.g., anchors, hatches, rudders, oars, etc.)
2050	Buoys
2090	Miscellaneous Ship, Marine, and Commercial Fishing Equipment (includes sails, marine furniture, ladders, etc.)

Railway Equipment

2210	Locomotives
2220	Rail Cars
2230	Right-of-Way Construction and Maintenance EQuipment, Railroad

2240	Locomotive and Rail Car Accessories and Components
2250	Track Materials, Railroad (e.g., rails, frogs, fish plats, etc.)

Motor Vehicles, Trailers and Cycles

2310A	Passenger sedans/station wagons
2310B	Ambulances and Hearses
2310C	Buses
2320A	Trucks and Truck Tractors one ton and heavier capacity
2320B	AMphibian Vehicles
2320C	Jeeps and all four-wheel drive vehicles of less than one ton capacity
2320D	Trucks with two-wheel drive of less than one ton capacity
2330	Trailers (e.g., semitrailers, house trailers, semitrailer dollies, etc.)
2340	Motorcycles, Motor Scooters, and Bicycles

Tractors

2410	Tractors, Full Track, Low Speed (e.g., caterpillar and crawler, etc.)
2420	Tractors, Wheeled (e.g., agricultural and industrial wheeled tractors, etc.)
2430	Tractors, Track Laying, High Speed

Vehicular Equipment Components

2510	Vehicular Cab, Body and Frame Structural Components
2520	Vehicular Power Transmission Components
2530	Vehicular Brake, Steering, Axles, Wheel, and Track Components
2540	Vehicular Furniture and Accessories
2590	Miscellaneous Vehicular Components (e.g., A-frames, bulldozer blades, crane booms, etc.)

Tires and Tubes

2610	Tires and Tubes, Pneumatic, except Aircraft
2620	Tires and Tubes, Pneumatic, Aircraft
2630	Tires, Solid and Cushion (includes rubber track laying treads
2640	Tire Rebuilding and Tire and Tube Repair Materials/Machinery

Engines, Turbines and Components

2805	Gasoline Reciprocating Engines, except Aircraft; and Components
2810	Gasoline Reciprocating Engines, Aircraft; and Components (e.g., only aircraft prime mover types)
2815	Diesel Engines and Components
2820	Steam Engines, Reciprocating and Components
2825	Steam Turbines and Components
2835	Gas Turbines and Jet Engines, except Aircraft; and Components (e.g. airborne auxiliary and ground gas turbine power units for aircraft engine starting, etc.)
2840	Gas Turbines and Jet Engines, Aircraft and Components
2845	Rocket Engines and Components
2895	Miscellaneous Compressed Air and Wind Engines; Water Turbines and Wheels; and Components

Engine Accessories

2910	Engine Fuel System Components, Non-aircraft
2915	Engine Fuel System Components, Aircraft
2920	Engine Electrical System Components, Non-aircraft
2925	Engine Electrical System Components, Aircraft
2930	Engine Cooling Systems Components, Non-aircraft
2935	Engine Cooling Systems Component, Aircraft
2940	Engine Air and Oil Filters, Strainers, and Cleaners, Non-aircraft
2945	Engine Air and Oil Filters, Strainers, and Cleaners, Aircraft
2950	Turbosuperchargers
2990	Miscellaneous Engine Accessories, Non-aircraft
2995	Miscellaneous Engine Accessories, Aircraft

Mechanical Power Transmission Equipment

3010	Torque Converters and Speed Changers
3020	Gears, Pulleys, Sprockets, and Transmission Chain
3030	Belting, Drive Belts, Fan Belts and Accessories
3040	Miscellaneous Power Transmission Equipment

Bearings

3110	Bearings, Antifriction, Unmounted
3120	Bearings, Plain, Unmounted
3130	Bearings, Mounted

Woodworking Machinery and Equipment

3210	Sawmill and Planing Mill Machinery
3220	Woodworking Machines (excludes hand held power driven tools)
3230	Tools and Attachments for Woodworking Machinery

Metalworking Machinery

3411	Boring Machines
3412	Broaching Machines
3413	Drilling and Tapping Machines
3414	Gear Cutting and Finishing Machines
3415	Grinding Machines
3416	Lathes (excludes speed lathes)
3417	Milling Machines
3418	Planers and Shapers
3419	Miscellaneous Machine Tools (e.g. gun rifling machines, speed lathes, etc.)
3422	Rolling Mills and Drawing Machines
3424	Metal Heat Treating and Non-Thermal Treating Equipment
3426	Metal Finishing Equipment
3431	Electric Arc Welding Equipment (excludes welding supplies and associated equipment)
3432	Electric Resistance Welding Equipment
3433	Gas Welding, Heat Cutting and Metalizing Equipment
3436	Welding Positioners and Manipulators
3438	Miscellaneous Welding Equipment

3439	Miscellaneous Welding, Soldering and Brazing Supplies and Accessories
3441	Bending and Forming Machines
3442	Hydraulic and Pneumatic Presses, Power Driven
3443	Mechanical Presses, Power Driven (includes forging presses)
3444	Manual Presses
3445	Punching and Shearing Machines
3446	Forging Machinery and Hammers (excludes forging presses)
3447	Wire and Metal Ribbon Forming Machines (excludes roll forming machines
3448	Riveting Machines (excludes power driven hand riveting machines)
3449	Miscellaneous Secondary Metal Forming and Cutting Machines
3450	Machine Tools, Portable
3455	Cutting Tools for Machine Tools (excludes flame cutting tools)
3456	Cutting and Forming Tools for Secondary Metalworking Machinery)
3460	Machine Tool Accessories
3465	Production Jigs, Fixtures and Templates
3470	Machine Shop Sets, Kits and Outfits

Service and Trade Equipment

3510	Laundry and Dry Cleaning Equipment
3520	Shoe Repairing Equipment
3530	Industrial Sewing Machines and Mobile Textile Repair Shops (excludes shoe sewing machines)
3540	Wrapping and Packaging Machinery
3550	Vending and Coin Operated Machines
3590	Miscellaneous Service and Trade Equipment (includes barber chairs, kits, hair clippers and shears, etc.

Special Industry Machinery

3605	Food Products Machinery and Equipment (excludes kitchen and galley equipment)
3610	Printing, Duplicating and Bookbinding Equipment
3615	Pulp and Paper Industries Machinery
3620	Rubber and Plastics Working Machinery
3625	Textile Industries Machinery
3635	Crystal and Glass Industries Machinery
3645	Leather Tanning and Leather Working Industries Machinery
3650	Chemical and Pharmaceutical Products Manufacturing Machinery
3655	Gas Generating Equipment (excludes meteorological equipment)
3680	Foundry Machinery, Related Equipment and Supplies (e.g., molding machines, tumbling mills, foundry dextrine, core paste, etc.)
3685	Specialized Metal Container Manufacturing Machinery and Related Equipment
3690	Specialized Ammunition and Ordnance Machinery and Related Equipment
3695	Miscellaneous Special Industry Machinery

Agricultural Machinery and Equipment

3710	Soil Preparation Equipment
3720	Harvesting Equipment

3740	Pest, Disease and Frost Control Equipment
3750	Gardening Implements and Tools

Construction, Mining, Excavating and Highway Maintenance Equipment

3805	Earth Moving and Excavating Equipment
3810	Cranes and Crane-Shovels (excludes barge-mounted cranes)
3815	Crane and Crane-Shovel Attachments
3820	Mining, Rock Drilling, Earth Boring, and Related Equipment
3825	Road Cleaning and Cleaning Equipment
3830	Truck and Tractor Attachments (e.g., augers, blades, sweepers, etc.)
3835	Petroleum Production and Distribution Equipment (includes wellheads, pumping equipment, and gas distribution equipment)
3895	Miscellaneous Construction Equipment (e.g., asphalt heaters and kettles, concrete mixers, pile drivers, cable laying, lashing, spinning and reeling equipment, etc.)

Materials Handling Equipment

3910	Conveyors
3920	Material Handling Equipment, Nonself-Propelled (e.g., hand trucks and material handling trailers)
3930	Warehouse Trucks and Tractors, Self-Propelled
3940	Blocks, Tackle, Rigging and Slings
3950	Winches, Hoists, Cranes, and Derricks
3960	Elevators and Escalators
3990	Miscellaneous Materials Handling Equipment (e.g., skids/pallets)

Rope, Cable, Chain and Fittings

4010	Chain and Wire Rope
4020	Fiber Rope, Cordage and Twine
4030	Fittings for Rope, Cable and Chain

Refrigeration and Air Conditioning Equipment

4110	Self-Contained Refrigeration Units and and Accessories
4120	Self-Contained Air Conditioning Units and Accessories
4130	Refrigeration and Air Conditioning Plants and Components
4140	Fans and Air Circulators, Nonindustrial

Fire Fighting, Rescue and Safety Equipment

4210	Fire Fighting Equipment (including fire trucks)
4220	Marine Lifesaving and Diving Equipment (excludes lifesaving boats)
4230	Decontaminating and Impregnating Equipment
4240	Safety and Rescue Equipment

Pumps and Compressors

4310	Compressors and Vacuum Pumps
4320	Power and Hand Pumps
4330	Centrifugals Separators and Pressure and Vacuum Filters

Furnace, Steam Plant and Drying Equipment

4410   Industrial Blower
4420   heat Exchangers and Steam Condensers
4430   Industrial Furnaces, Kilns, Lehs and Ovens (excludes food industry ovens, metal heat treating and laboratory type furnaces)
4440   Driers, Dehydrators and Anhydrators
4450   Industrial Fan and Blower Equipment
4460   Air Purification Equipment

Plumbing, Heating and Sanitation Equipment

4510   Plumbing Fixtures and Accessories
4520   Space heating Equipment and Domestic Water Heaters
4530   Fuel Burning Equipment Units
4540   Miscellaneous Plumbing, Heating and Sanitation Equipment

Water Purification and Sewage Treatment Equipment

4610   Water Purification Equipment
4620   Water Distillation Equipment Equipment, Marine and Industrial
4630   Sewage Treatment Equipment

Pipe, Tubing, Hose and Fittings

4710   Pipe and Tube (for other than underground, electrical or laboratory use)
4720   Hose and Tubing, Flexible (e.g., hose and tubing, hydraulic, air, chemical, fuel and oil hose assemblies)
4730   Fittings and Specialties

Valves

4810   Valves, Powered
4820   Valves, Nonpowered

Maintenance and Repair Shop Equipment

4910   Motor Vehicle Maintenance and Repair Shop Specialized Equipment (excludes hand tools)

4920   Aircraft Maintenance and Repair Shop Specialized Equipment
4925   Ammunition Maintenance and Repair Shop Specialized Equipment
4930   Lubrication and Fuel Dispensing Equipment
4931   Fire Control Maintenance and Repair Shop Specialized Equipment
4933   Weapons Maintenance and Repair Shop Specialized Equipment
4935   Guided Missile Maintenance, Repair, and Checkout Specialized Equipment
4940   Miscellaneous Maintenance and Repair Shop Specialized Equipment (includes paint spraying equipment)
4960   Space Vehicle Maintenance, Repair and Checkout Specialized Equipment

Hand Tools

5110	Hand Tools, Edged, Nonpowered
5120	Hand Tools, Nonedged, Nonpowered
5130	Hand Tools, Power Driven
5133	Drill Bits, Counterbores, and Countersinks: Hand and Machine
5136	Taps, Dies and Colleges: Hand and Machine (excludes punching, stamping and marking dies)
5140	Tool and Hardware Boxes
5180	Sets, Kits and Outfits of Hand Tools

Measuring Tools

5210	Measuring Tools, Craftsmen's
5220	Inspection Gages and Precision Layout Tools
5280	Sets, Kits and Outfits of Measuring Tools

Hardware and Abrasives

5305	Screws
5306	Bolts
5307	Studs
5310	Nuts and Washers
5315	Nails, keys and Pins
5320	Rivets
5330	Packing and Basket Materials
5340	Miscellaneous Hardware and Metal Screening
5345	Disks and Stones, Abrasive
5350	Abrasive Materials
5355	Knobs and Pointers

Prefabricated Structures and Scaffolding

5410	Prefabricated and Portable Buildings
5420	Bridges, Fixed and Floating (excludes pontoons and floating docks)
5430	Storage Tanks
5440	Scaffolding Equipment and Concrete Forms
5455	Prefabricated Tower Structures
5450	Miscellaneous Prefabricated Structures (e.g., bleachers)

Lumber, Millwork, Plywood and Veneer

5510	Lumber and Related Basic Wood Materials (e.g., plywood)

Construction and Building Materials

5610	Mineral Construction Materials, Bulk
5640	Wallboard, Building Paper, and Thermal Insulation Materials
5650	Roofing and Siding Materials
5660	Fencing, Fences, and Gates
5670	Architectural and Related Metal Products (e.g., door frames, fixed fire escapes, grating, staircases, window sash, etc.)
5680	Miscellaneous Construction Materials (e.g., metal lath, airplane landing mats, traction mats, tile, brick, nonmetallic pipe and conduit)

Communication Equipment

5805	Telephone and Telegraph Equipment
5815	Teletype and Facsimile Equipment
5820	Radio and Television Communication Equipment, except Airborne (excludes home-type radio and television equipment)
5821	Radio and Television Communication Equipment, Airborne
5825	Radio Navigation Equipment, except Airborne
5826	Radio Navigation Equipment, Airborne
5830	Intercommunication and Public Address System, except Airborne
5831	Intercommunication and Public Address System, Airborne
5835	Sound Recording and Reproducing Equipment (excludes phonographs, home-type, and dictation machines)
5840	Radar Equipment, except Airborne
5841	Radar Equipment, Airborne
5845	Underwater Sound Equipment (includes only communication types of infrared equipment)
5895	Miscellaneous Communication Equipment

Electrical and Electronic Equipment Components

5905	Resistors
5910	Capacitors
5915	Filters and Networks
5920	Fuses and Lightning Arresters
5925	Circuit Breakers
5930	Switches
5935	Connectors, Electrical
5940	Lugs, Terminals, and Terminal Strips
5945	Relays, Contractors, and Solenoids
5950	Coils and Transformers
5955	Piezoelectric Crystals
5960	Electron Tubes
5961	Semi-Conductor Devices and Associated Hardware
5965	Headsets, Handsets, Microphones, and Speakers
5970	Electrical Insulators and Insulating Materials
5975	Electrical Hardware and Supplies
5977	Electrical Contact Bruhes and Electrodes
5985	Antennas, Waveguides, and Related Equipment
5990	Synchros and Resolvers (includes autosyn motors, selsyn generators, synchro receivers, torque amplifiers, etc.)
5995	Cable, Cord and Wire Assemblies: Communication Equipment
5999	Miscellaneous Electrical and Electronic Components

Electric Wire and Power and Distribution Equipment

6105	Motors, Electrical
6110	Electrical Control Equipment
6115	Generators and Generator Sets, Electrical
6120	Transformers: Distribution and Power Station
6125	Converters, Electrical
6130	Power Conversion Equipment, Electrical
6135	Batteries, Primary

6140	Batteries, Secondary
6145	Wire and Cable, Electrical
6150	Miscellaneous Electric Power and Distribution Equipment

Lighting Fixtures and Lamps

6210	Indoor and Outdoor Electric Lighting Fixtures
6220	Electric Vehicular Lights and Fixtures (includes railroad and aircraft fixtures)
6230	Electric Portable and Hand Lighting Equipment
6240	Electric Lamps
6250	Ballasts, Lampholders, and Starters

Alarm and Signal Systems

6320	Shipboard Alarm and Signal Systems
6340	Aircraft Alarm and Signal Systems
6350	Miscellaneous Alarm and Signal Systems

Medical, Dental and Veterinary Equipment and Supplies

6505	Drugs, Biologicals and Official Reagents
6510	Surgical Dressing Materials
6515	Medical and Surgical Instruments, Equipment and Supplies
6520	Dental Instruments, Equipment and Supplies
6525	X-Ray Equipment and Supplies
6530	Hospital Furniture, Equipment, Utensils, and Supplies
6540	Opticians' Instruments, Equipment and Supplies
6545	Medical Sets, Kits and Outfits

Instruments and Laboratory Equipment

6605	Navigational Instruments
6610	Flight Instruments
6615	Automatic Pilot Mechanisms and Airborne Gyro Components
6620	Engine Instruments (includes all aircraft, marine, and vehicular engine instruments)
6625	Electrical and Electronic Properties Measuring and Testing Instruments
6630	Chemical Analysis Instruments (e.g., gas analyzers, hydrometers, etc.)
6635	Physical Properties Testing Equipment (e.g., balancing machines, industrial X-ray machines, torque bearing testers, etc.)
6636	Environmental Chambers and Related Equipment
6640	Laboratory Equipment and Supplies
6645	Time Measuring Instruments
6650	Optical Instruments
6655	Geophysical and Astronomical Instruments
6660	Meteorological Instruments and Apparatus
6665	Hazard-Detecting Instruments and Apparatus
6670	Scales and Balances
6675	Drafting, Surveying, and Mapping Instruments
6680	Liquid and Gas Flow, Liquid Level, and Mechanical Motion Measuring Instruments

6685   Pressure, Temperature and Humidity Measuring and Controlling Instruments

6695   Combination and Miscellaneous Instruments (e.g., lie detectors, meter registers, etc.)

Photographic Equipment

6710   Cameras, Motion Picture
6720   Cameras, Still Picture
6730   Photographic Projection Equipment
6740   Photographic Developing and Finishing Equipment
6750   Photographic Supplies
6760   Photographic Equipment and Accessories
6770   Film, Processed
6780   Photographic Sets, Kits and Outfits

Chemicals and Chemical Products

6810   Chemicals (includes nonmedicinal chemical elements and compounds, such as naphtha solvents, acetone, etc.)
6830   Gases: Compressed and Liquefied
6840   Pest Control Agents and Disinfectants
6850   Miscellaneous Chemical Specialties (e.g., antifogging compound, antifreeze, deicing fluid, etc.)

Training Aids and Devices

6910   Training Aids (e.g., cutaway models, vehicle training aids, etc.)
6920   Armament Training Devices (e.g., silhouette targets, etc.)
6930   Operational Training Devices (e.g., flight simulators, etc.)
6940   Communication Training Devices

Furniture

7105   Household Furniture
7110   Office Furniture
7125   Cabinets, Lockers, Bins, and Shelving
7195   Miscellaneous Furniture and Fixtures

Household and Commercial Furnishings and Appliances

7210   Household Furnishings (e.g., bed blankets, mattresses, and pillows, etc.
7240   Household and Commercial Utility Containers
7290   Miscellaneous Household and Commercial Furnishings and Appliances (e.g., carpets, tile, draperies, awnings, etc.

Food Preparation and Serving Equipment

7310   Food Cooking, Baking and Warming Equipment
7320   Kitchen Equipment and Appliances
7330   Kitchen Hand Tools and Utensils
7350   Tableware
7360   Sets, Kits and Outfits: Food Preparation and Serving

Office Machines and Data Processing Equipment

7410   Punched Card System Machines
7420   Accounting and Calculating Machines
7430   Typewriters and Office Type Composing Machines
7440   Automatic Data Processing Systems: Industrial, Scientific and Office Types
7450   Office Type Sound Recording and Reproducing Machines
7460   Visible Record Equipment (e.g., rotary files, etc.)
7490   Miscellaneous Office Machines (e.g., cash registers, check machines, label printing machines, etc.)

Office Supplies and Devices

7510   Office Supplies
7520   Office Devices and Accessories
7530   Stationery and Record Forms (excludes standard forms approved for Government-wide use)

Books and Other Publications

7610   Books and Pamphlets

Musical Instruments, Phonographs and Home-Type Radios

7710   Musical Instruments and Accessories
7730   Phonographs, Radios, and Television Sets: Home-Type

Recreational and Athletic Equipment

7810   Athletic and Sporting Equipment
7830   Recreational and Gymnastic Equipment

Cleaning Equipment and Supplies

7910   Floor Polishers and Vacuum Cleaners
7930   Cleaning and Polishing Compounds and Preparations

Brushes, Paints, Sealers and Adhesives

8010   Paints, Dopes, Varnishes, and Related Products
8030   Preservative and Sealing Compounds
8040   Adhesives

Containers, Packaging and Packing Supplies

8105   Bags and Sacks
8110   Drums and Cans
8115   Boxes, Cartons, and Crates
8120   Gas Cylinders
8125   Bottles and Jars
8130   Reels and Spools
8135   Packaging and Packing Bulk Materials (e.g., baling wire, waterproof barriers, corrugated and wrapping paper, etc.)

8140   Ammunition and Nuclear Ordnance Boxes, Packages, and Special Containers
8145   Shipping and Storage Containers

Textiles, Leather, Furs, Apparel and Shoe Findings, Tents and Flags

8305B   Textile Fabrics
8340   Tents and Tarpaulins

Clothing and Individual Equipment

8405   Outerwear, Men's
8410   Outerwear, Women's
8415   Clothing, Special Purpose, Safety, Protective, and Athletic
8420   Underwear and Nightwear, Men's
8430   Footwear, Men's
8435   Footwear, Women's
8440   Hosiery, Handwear and Clothing Accessories: Men's
8445   Hosiery, Handwear and Clothing Accessories: Women's
8460   Luggage
8465   Individual Equipment (e.g., ammunition belts, intrenching tool carriers, sleeping and duffel bags, flying goggles, sun glasses, etc.)
8475   Specialized Flight Clothing and Accessories

Agricultural Supplies

8710   Forage and Feed

Live Animals

8820   Live Animals

Fuels, Lubricants, Oils, and Waxes

9110   Fuels, Solid
9130   Liquid Propellants and Fuels, Petroleum Base
9135   Liquid Propellant Fuels and Oxidizers, Chemical Base
9140   Fuel Oils
9150   Oils and Greases: Cutting, Lubricating, and Hydraulic
9160   Miscellaneous Waxes, Oils, and Fats

Nonmetallic Fabricated Materials

9310   Paper and Paperboard
9320   Rubber Fabricated Materials
9330   Plastics Fabricated Materials
9340   Glass Fabricated Materials
9350   Refractories and Fire Surfacing Materials
9390   Miscellaneous Fabricated Nonmetallic Materials (e.g., asbestos fabricated materials, cork and fibre sheets, etc.)

Metal Bars, Sheets, and Shapes

9505	Wire, nonelectrical, Iron and Steel
9510	Bars and Rods, Iron and Steel
9515	Plate, Sheet and Strip: Iron and Steel
9520	Structural Shapes, Iron and Steel
9525	Wire, Nonelectrical, Nonferrous Base Metal
9530	Bars and Rods, Nonferrous Base Metal
9535	Plate, Sheet, Strip and Foil: Nonferrous Base Metal
9540	Structural Shapes, Nonferrous Base Metal
9545	Plate, Sheet, Strip, Foil, and Wire: Precious Metal

Primary Metal Products

9630	Additive Metal Materials and Master Alloys
9640	Iron and Steel Primary and Semifinished Products (e.g., ingots, pigs, billets, blooms, muck bar, skelp, rods for wire, sheet bar, etc.)
9650	Nonferrous Base Metal Refinery and Intermediate Forms (e.g., ingots, slabs, mercury, etc.)

APPENDIX 2

SOME LOCATIONS OF PAST DoD SALES

The following list is to give you an example of how varied and numerous are the locations at which DoD auctions are held. Please remember that this is only a **partial list;** there will doubtless be even more locations, some perhaps very near to your home.

Physical Location	City	State
Eilson AFB	Fairbanks	AK
Elmendorf AFB	Anchorage	AK
Fort Wainwright	Fairbanks	AK
Naval Station	Adak	AK
Alabama Army Ammo Plant	Childersburg	AL
Brookely AFB	Mobile	AL
Craig AFB	Selma	AL
DRMO Anniston, Bldg 5274	Anniston	AL
DRMO Huntsville, Bldg 7408	Redstone Arsnl	AL
DRMO Montgomery, Bldg 900	Montgomery	AL
DRMO Rucker, Bldg 1313	Fort Rucker	AL
Fort McClellan, Bldg T342	Anniston	AL
Maxwell AFB, Bldg 900	Montgomery	AL
US Army State Docks	Mobile	AL
US Property & Fiscal Ofc	Maxwell AFB	AL
Blytheville AFB	Blytheville	AR
Camp Chaffee, Bldg 339	Fort Smith	AR
DRMO Little Rock, Bldg 1575	Jacksonville	AR
Pine Bluff Arsenal	Pine Bluff	AR
Davis-Monthan AFB	Tucson	AZ
Fort Huachuca	Fort Huachuca	AZ
Gila Bend Gunnery Range	Gila Bend	AZ
Luke AFB	Glendale	AZ
Marine Corps Air Station	Yuma	AZ
Navajo Army Depot	Flagstaff	AZ
Williams AFB	Chandler	AZ
Yuma Proving Grounds	Yuma	AZ
Fort Irwin	Barstow	CA
Letterman Army Medical Center	San Francisco	CA
Fort MacArthur	San Pedro	CA
Oakland Army Base	Oakland	CA
Camp Roberts	San Miguel	CA
Riverbank Army Ammo Plant	Riverbank	CA
Rough and Ready Island	Stockton	CA
Sacramento Army Depot	Sacramento	CA
Fort Ord	Monterey	CA
Sierra Army Depot	Herlong	CA
US Coast Guard Training Ctr	Petaluma	CA
Mather AFB	Sacramento	CA

Defense Depot Tracy	Tracy	CA
George AFB	Victorville	CA
Edwards AFB	Edwards	CA
Mira Loma AFB	Mira Loma	CA
Federal Service Center	Bell	CA
R&R Island-DIPEC Project	Stockton	CA
Sharpe Army Depot	Lathrop	CA
March AFB	Riverside	CA
Beale AFB	Marysville	CA
Norton AFB	San Bernardino	CA
Castle AFB	Merced	CA
Hamilton AFB	Ignatio	CA
McClellan AFB	Sacramento	CA
Travis AFB	Fairfield	CA
Vandenburg AFB	Lompoc	CA
Naval Air Station	Alameda	CA
NAS Lemoore	Lemoore	CA
NAS Moffett Field	Sunnyvale	CA
Alameda Facility	Alameda	CA
Navl Weapons Station	Seal Beach	CA
MCLB Barstow	Barstow	CA
MCB Pendleton	Oceanside	CA
Mare Island Annx NWS Concord	Vallejo	CA
Concord Nav Weapons Station	Concord	CA
Naval Weapons Center	China Lake	CA
NAS Point Mugu	Point Mugu	CA
Pt Molate Annex NSC Oakland	Richmond	CA
Naval Air Facility	El Centro	CA
Naval Electronics Lab	San Diego	CA
Marine Corps Air Faiclity	Santa Ana	CA
Naval Weapons Station	Fallbrook	CA
Naval Hospital	Oceanside	CA
Naval Regional Medical Ctr	Oakland	CA
OLF, Imperial Beach	Imperial Beach	CA
Naval Air Station	Los Alamitos	CA
Naval Supply Center Annex	Torrance	CA
Naval Shipyard	Long Beach	CA
OSB Long Beach	Terminal Island	CA
MCAS El Toro	East Irvine	CA
Naval Amphibious Base	Coronado	CA
Marine Corps Recruit Depot	San Diego	CA
Naval Station	National City	CA
North Island NAS	San Diego	CA
NOL Corona	Corona	CA
Naval Supply Center	Oakland	CA
NCBC, Port Hueneme	Port Hueneme	CA
Presidio of San Francisco	San Francisco	CA
Naval Air Station	Miramar	CA
Naval Supply Center	San Diego	CA
Hunters Point NSY	San Francisco	CA
Mare Island NSY	Vallejo	CA
Marine Corps Base	29 Palms	CA
Naval Training Center	San Diego	CA
Naval Sta-Treasure Island	San Francisco	CA

Buckley AFB	Denver	CO
Fort Carson	Colorado Spgs	CO
Pueblo Army Depot	Pueblo	CO
Rocky Mountain Arsenal	Commerce City	CO
Fitzsimons Army Hospital	Denver	CO
Air Force Academy	Colorado Spgs	CO
Lowry AFB	Denver	CO
ENT AFB	Colorado Spgs	CO
DRMO Groton, NSB New London	Groton	CT
Harry Diamond Lab	Washington	DC
Fort Leslie J. McNair	Washington	DC
Army Map Service	Washington	DC
Naval Research Laboratory	Washington	DC
Washington Navy Yard	Washington	DC
7th Coast Guard District	Miami	FL
DRMO Eglin, Bldg 525	Eglin AFB	FL
DRMO Patrick, Bldg 1391	Patrick AFB	FL
DRMO Homestead, Bldg 607	Homestead AFB	FL
Tyndall AFB, Bldg 6027	Panama City	FL
DRMO Tampa, Bldg 1110	Tampa	FL
Cape Canaveral AS, Bldg 66615	Cape Canaveral	FL
Avon Park Gunnery Range	Avon Park	FL
McCoy AFB	Orlando	FL
Naval Air Station, Bldg 795	Key West	FL
Navy Coastal Systems Lab	Panama City	FL
DRMO Pensacola, Bldg 685N	Pensacola	FL
DRMO Jacksonville, Bldg 174D	Jacksonville	FL
NAS - Cecil Field, Bldg 179	Jacksonville	FL
Navy Fuel Depot	Jacksonville	FL
DRMO Key West, Bldg 795	Key West	FL
Naval Station, Bldg 412	Mayport	FL
Navpltbr Pratt-Whitney Acft	West Palm Beach	FL
DRMO Orlando, Bldg 1063	Orlando	FL
Naval Aux Air Sta-Whiting	Pensacola	FL
Naval Comm Trn Ctr/Corry Fld	Pensacola	FL
Navy Hel Trn/Ellyson Field	Pensacola	FL
Fort Gillem, Bldg 310B	Forest Park	GA
DRMO Benning, Bldg 467	Columbus	GA
DRMO Gordon, Bldg 10601	Fort Gordon	GA
Fort McPherson	Fort McPherson	GA
Hunter Army Airfield	Savannah	GA
DRMO Stewart, Bldg 1525	Hinesville	GA
Mil Ocean Terminal-Kings Bay	Kingsland	GA
Dobbins AFB	Marietta	GA
Moody AFB, Bldg 997	Valdosta	GA
Travis Field	Savannah	GA
US Naval Air Station	Brunswick	GA
DRMO Albany, Bldg 1331	Albany	GA

Navy Sub Supply Base	Kings Bay	GA
Nav Ex-Nav Sup Corps School	Athens	GA
DRMO Hawaii	Pearl Harbor	HI
Air National Guard	Des Moines	IA
Army National Guard	Des Moines	IA
Iowa Army Ammo Plant	Middleton	IA
Gowan Field	Boise	ID
Mountain Home AFB	Mountain Home	ID
DCASR Chicago Ohare IAP	Chicago	IL
DRMO Rock Island Arsenal	Rock Island	IL
DRMO Chanute	Chanute AFB	IL
DRMO Scott	Scott AFB	IL
DRMO Great Lakes Nav Trn Ctr	Great Lakes	IL
Fort Sheridan	Fort Sheridan	IL
Granite City Army Dep	Granite City	IL
Joliet Army Ammo Plant	Joliet	IL
Savanna Army Depot, Site S	Savanna	IL
Crane Army Ammunition Act	Crane	IN
DIPEF	Terre Haute	IN
DRMO Indianapolis	Ft. Ben Harrison	IN
Grissom AFB	Grissom AFB	IN
Indiana Army Ammo Plant	Charlestown	IN
Jefferson Proving Ground	Madison	IN
Naval Avionics Facilities	Indianapolis	IN
Newport Army Ammo Plant	Newport	IN
DIPEF	Atchison	KS
DIPEF-DIPEC Project	Atchison	KS
DRMO Riley	Fort Riley	KS
Forbes ANG	Topeka	KS
Fort Leavenworth, Site L	Ft. Leavenworth	KS
Kansas Army Ammo Plant	Parsons	KS
McConnell AFB, Site M	McConnell AFB	KS
Naval Air Station	Olathe	KS
Sunflower Army Ammo Plant	Desoto	KS
Blue Grass Activity	Richmond	KY
DRMO Campbell, Bldg 5212	Fort Campbell	KY
DRMO Knox	Fort Knox	KY
DRMO Lexington, Bldg 17E	Lexington	KY
US Naval Ord Plant	Louisville	KY
Barksdale AFB, Bldg 4964	Shreveport	LA
Camp Beauregard	Alexandria	LA
DRMO Polk Bldg 4050	Fort Polk	LA
England AFB, Bldg 2515	Alexandria	LA
HQ Support Act, 8th Nav Dist	New Orleans	LA
Louisiana Army Ammo Plant	Shreveport	LA
Naval Air Station	Belle Chase	LA

Naval Air Station Algiers	New Orleans	LA
New Orleans	New Orleans	LA
DRMO Ayer	Fort Devens	MA
DRMO Chicopee Falls	Westover AFB	MA
First Coast Guard District	Boston	MA
Hanscom Field	Bedford	MA
Naval Shipyard	Boston	MA
Naval Air Station	South Weymouth	MA
Otis ANGB	Otis ANGB	MA
Watertown Arsenal	Watertown	MA
A G Publishing Center	Baltimore	MD
Andrews Air Force Base	Andrews AFB	MD
David Taylor Naval Ship R&D	Bethesda	MD
DRMO Brandywine	Brandywine	MD
DRMO Meade	Fort Meade	MD
DRMO Aberdeen	Aberdeen Pr Gnd	MD
Edgewood Arsenal	Edgewood	MD
Fort Holabird	Baltimore	MD
Naval Academy	Annapolis	MD
Naval Ship R&D Center	Annapolis	MD
Naval Surface Weapons Ctr	Silver Springs	MD
US Coast Guard	Baltimore	MD
US Naval Training Center	Bainbridge	MD
Coast Guard Base	South Portland	ME
Dow AFB	Dow AFB	ME
DRMO Limestone	Loring AFB	ME
DRMO Brunswick Nav Air Sta	Brunswick	ME
Camp Grayling	Grayling	MI
Chrysler Arsenal Tank Plant	Warren	MI
DLSC-Federal Center	Battle Creek	MI
DRMO Sawyer	K I Sawyer AFB	MI
DRMO Detroit, Selfridge	Selfridge	MI
DRMO Wurtsmith	Wurtsmith AFB	MI
Fort Custer	Battle Creek	MI
Kincheloe AFB	Kincheloe AFB	MI
Material Readiness Command	Warren	MI
Michigan Army Missle Plant	Sterling Heights	MI
Pontiac Storage Facility	Pontiac	MI
Pont Strg Fac-DIPEC Project	Pontiac	MI
US Coast Guard Air Station	Traverse City	MI
Camp Ripley	Little Falls	MN
DRMO Duluth	Duluth	MN
Twin Cities Army Ammo Plant	New Brighton	MN
A F Aero Chart & Info Ctr	St. Louis	MO
DRMO Leonard Wood	Ft. Leonard Wood	MO
DRMO Whiteman	Whiteman AFB	MO
Fort Richie	Cascade	MO
Gateway Army Ammo Plant	St. Louis	MO

Lake City Army Ammo Plant	Independence	MO
Richards Gebaur AFB	Rich Gebaur AFB	MO
St. Louis Procurement Dist	St. Louis	MO
USA-AG Publications Center	St. Louis	MO
Army Engineers Experiment St	Vicksburg	MS
Columbus AFB, Bldg 152	Columbus	MS
DRMO Keesler, Bldg 4422	Keesler AFB	MS
Naval Auxiliary Air Station	Meridian	MS
Nav Const Bat Center	Gulfport	MS
USP&FO for Miss, Bldg 6520	Hattisburg	MS
Fort Wm Henry Harrison	Helena	MT
Malmstrom AFB	Great Falls	MT
Navy and MC Reserve Trn Ctr	Butte	MT
NSMCR Training Center	Great Falls	MT
Charlotte Army Missile Plant	Charlotte	NC
Coast Guard Station	Elizabeth City	NC
DRMO Bragg, Bldg J1334	Fort Bragg	NC
DRMO Cherry Point, Bldg 154D	Havelock	NC
DRMO LeJeune, Bldg 906	Camp LeJeune	NC
Military Ocean Terminal	Southport	NC
Pope AFB	Fort Bragg	NC
Rosman Research Station	Rosman	NC
Seymour Johnson AFB, Bldg 2620	Goldsboro	NC
Minot AFB	Minot	ND
Cornhusker Army Ammo Plant	Grand Island	NE
DRMO Offutt	Offutt AFB	NE
Lincoln Army National Guard	Lincoln	NE
DRMO Portsmouth, NSY	Portsmouth	NH
Pease AFB	Pease AFB	NH
Burlington Army Ammo Plant	Burlington	NJ
DRMO Bayonne	Bayonne	NJ
DRMO Lakehurst, Nav Air Eng	Lakehurst	NJ
DRMO McGuire AFB	Wrightstown	NJ
DRMS-RPE	Colts Neck	NJ
Fort Dix	Fort Dix	NJ
Fort Monmouth	Red Bank	NJ
Naval Air Turbine Test Sta	Trenton	NJ
Naval Supply Center	Bayonne	NJ
Naval Weapons Station Earle	Colts Neck	NJ
US Arracom	Dover	NJ
US Coast Guard Station	Sandy Hook	NJ
White Sands Missile Range	Alamogordo	NM
Fort Wingate	Gallup	NM
Cannon AFB	Clovis	NM
Holloman AFB	Alamogordo	NM

Kirtland AFB	Alburquerque	NM
Oscura Gunnery Range	Alamogordo	NM
Hawthorne Army Ammunition Pt	Hawthorne	NV
Hawthorne Army Ammo Plant	Hawthorne	NV
Indian Springs AFB	Indian Springs	NV
Naval Auxiliary Air Station	Fallon	NV
Nellis AFB	Las Vegas	NV
Naval Ammo Depot	Hawthorne	NV
Coast Guard Base	Staten Island	NY
DRMO Watervliet	Watervliet	NY
DRMO Rome	Griffis AFB	NY
DRMO Plattsburg	Plattsburg AFB	NY
Fort Drum	Fort Drum	NY
Fort Tilden	Queens	NY
Fort Wadsworth	Staten Island	NY
Grumman Aerospace-Navpro	Bethpage	NY
Hancock Field	Syracuse	NY
Naval Hospital	St. Albans	NY
Niagara Air Base Group	Niagara Falls	NY
Seneca AD-DIPEC Project	Romulus	NY
US Military Academy	West Point	NY
US Coast Guard Support Ctr	Governors Island	NY
763rd Radar Station	Lockport	NY
Defense Elect Supply Ctr	Dayton	OH
DRMO Bermuda	Bermuda	OH
DRMO Columbus DIPEC Project	Columbus	OH
DRMO Thule	Thule Air Base	OH
DRMO Wright Patterson	Wright Patt AFB	OH
Lima Army Modification Ctr	Lima	OH
Lima Army Tank Plant	Lima	OH
Naval Sta Guantanamo Bay	Cuba	OH
Newark Air Force Station	Heath	OH
Ninth Coast Guard District	Cleveland	OH
Ravenna Army Ammo Plant	Ravenna	OH
Rickenbacker ANG	Rickenbacker AB	OH
Seneca Army Depot	Port Clinton	OH
US Naval Facility	Argentia	OH
Altus AFB	Altus	OK
DRMO McAlester, Bldg 645	McAlester	OK
DRMO Oklahoma City, Bldg 3767	Oklahoma City	OK
DRMO Sill, Bldg 3323	Fort Sill	OK
Naval Ammo Depot	McAlester	OK
Vance AFB	Vance AFB	OK
Burns AFS-Radar Sqdn	Burns	OR
Coast Guard Base	Astoria	OR
Kingsley AFB	Klamath Falls	OR
Naval Facility Coos Head	Charleston	OR
Umatilla Army Depot	Hermiston	OR

Area Supply Office	Annville	PA
Carlisle Barracks	Carlisle	PA
Defense Depot Activity	Mechanicsburg	PA
DRMO Chambersburg, Ltr Kenny	Chambersburg	PA
DRMO Mechanicsburg	Mechanicsburg	PA
DRMO Philadelphia, DPSC	Philadelphia	PA
DRMO Tobyhanna	Tobyhanna	PA
Frankford Arsenal	Philadelphia	PA
HQ 911th Troop Carrier GP	Pittsburgh	PA
Marietta Air Force Station	Marietta	PA
Naval Air Sation	Willow Grove	PA
New Cumberland Army Depo	New Cumberland	PA
Scranton Army Ammo Plant	Scranton	PA
US Army Garr-Indiantown	Annville	PA
Coast Guard Base-La Puntilla	Old San Juan	PR
DRMO Roosevelt Rds, Bldg 745	Roosevelt Roads	PR
Fort Buchanan	Fort Buchanan	PR
US Navy Comm Sta Fort Allen	Ponce	PR
DRMO Davisville	Davisville	RI
Naval Education and Tng Ctr	Newport	RI
Charleston AFB	Charleston	SC
Charleston Army Depot	Charleston	SC
Charleston Naval Shipyard	Charleston	SC
Charleston Naval Station	Charleston	SC
DRMO Jackson, Bldg 1902	Fort Jackson	SC
Myrtle Beach AFB, Bldg 526	Myrtle Beach	SC
Marine Corp Air Station	Beaufort	SC
Nav Exch - Naval Station	Charleston	SC
Naval Weapons Station	Charleston	SC
Naval Weapons Station-Annex	Charleston	SC
Parris Island, Bldg 629	Parris Island	SC
SC State Ports Authority	N Charleston	SC
Army National Guard	Sioux Falls	SD
Ellsworth AFB	Rapid City	SD
Arnold Eng Dev Center	Arnold AFS	TN
DRMO Panama, Corozal	Panama	TN
DRMO Memphis, Bldg 2095	Memphis	TN
Holston Army Ammo Plant	Kingsport	TN
McGhee-Tyson Airport	Knoxville	TN
Milan Army Ammo Plant	Milan	TN
Naval Air Station, Bldg 262	Millington	TN
Volunteer Army Ammo Plant	Chattanooga	TN
Amarillo AFB	Amarillo	TX
Bergstrom AFB, Bldg 624	Austin	TX
Brooks AFB	San Antonio	TX
Camp Stanley	San Antonio	TX
DRMO Carswell, Bldg 1360	Carswell	TX
DRMO Corpus Christi, Bldg 22	Corpus Christi	TX

DRMO Dyess, Bldg 9102	Dyess AFB	TX
DRMO Hood, Bldg 4274	Fort Hood	TX
DRMO Laughlin AFB, Bldg T150	Del Rio	TX
DRMO San Antonio, Bldg 3000	East Kelly AFB	TX
DRMO Sheppard, Bldg 2135	Sheppard AFB	TX
DRMO Texarkana, Bldg 431	Hooks	TX
Ellington AFB	Houston	TX
Fort Bliss	EL Paso	TX
Fort Sam Houston	San Antonio	TX
Fort Wolters	Mineral Wells	TX
Goodfellow AFB	San Angelo	TX
Lackland AFB	Lackland AFB	TX
Lone Star Army Ammy Plant	Texarkana	TX
Lone Star Army Ammy Plant	Texarkana	TX
Longhorn Army Ammo Plant	Marshall	TX
Nav Aux Air Sta, Bldg 1701	Kingsville	TX
Nav Aux Air Sta, Bldg 109	Beeville	TX
Randolph AFB	San Antonio	TX
Reese AFB	Houston	TX
Webb AFB	Big Springs	TX
404th AF Base Squadron	Port O'Conner	TX
Defense Depot Ogden	Ogden	UT
Dugway Proving Ground	Dugway	UT
Fort Douglas	Salt Lake City	UT
Freeport Center	Clearfield	UT
Hercules Powder Co	Magna	UT
Hill AFB	Ogden	UT
Hill Bombing Range	Wendover	UT
Navy Oceanographic Office	Clearfield	UT
Utah Launch Complex	Green River	UT
Tooele Army Depot	Tooele	UT
Arlington Hall Station	Arlington	VA
Camp A. P. Hill	Fredericksburg	VA
Camp Pickett	Blackstone	VA
Coast Guard Reserve Trng Ctr	Yorktown	VA
DRMO Belvoir	Belvoir	VA
DRMO Richmond	Richmond	VA
Fort Eustis	Fort Eustis	VA
Fort Lee	Fort Lee	VA
Fort Myer	Arlington	VA
Fort Story	Virginia Beach	VA
Langley AFB	Langley AFB	VA
Naval AMPH Base-Little Creek	Norfolk	VA
Naval Air Station	Norfolk	VA
Naval Air Station-Oceana	Virgina Beach	VA
Naval FAAWTC-Dam Neck	Virginia Beach	VA
Naval Radio Station	Driver	VA
Naval Weapons Station	Yorktown	VA
Norfolk NSY-Salvage Yard	Portsmouth	VA
Radford Army Ammo Plant	Radford	VA
US Marine Corps Air Sta	Quantico	VA
US Naval Weapons Center	Dahlgren	VA

Fairchild AFB	Spokane	WA
Indian Island Detach	Hadlock	WA
Lewis Logistics Center	Tillicum	WA
McChord AFB	Tacoma	WA
NAS Whidbey Island	Oak Harbor	WA
Naval Ammo Depot Bangor	Bremerton	WA
Naval Facility	Pacific Beach	WA
Naval Support Activity	Seattle	WA
Puget Sound Naval Supply Ctr	Bremerton	WA
USN Torpedo St-Bangor Annex	Keyport	WA
Yakima Firing Center	Yakima	WA
13th Coast Guard District	Seattle	WA
Badger Army Ammo Plant	Baraboo	WI
DRMO Spart, Fort McCoy	Sparta	WI
Warren AFB	Cheyenne	WY

Overseas Locations (not a complete listing)

DRMO Guam	Agana	GU
DRMO Subic (Philippines)	Subic Bay	PI
DRMO Clark	Angeles	PI
DRMO Sagami	Sagami	JA
DRMO Iwakuni	Iwakuni	JA
DRMO Misawa	Misawa AFB	JA
DRMO Thailand	Bangkok	TH
DRMO Okinawa	Mikiminato	JA
DRMO Australia	Holt Exmouth	AT

APPENDIX 3

SMALL BUSINESS ADMINISTRATION OFFICES

To help you find the SBA office nearest to you, look for your state on the following list. Note which region your state is in, then see the list on the following pages for district and regional offices in your area.

Alabama	Region 4
Alaska	Region 10
Arizona	Region 9
Arkansas	Region 6
California	Region 9
Colorado	Region 8
Connecticut	Region 1
Delaware	Region 3
District of Columbia	Region 3
Florida	Region 4
Georgia	Region 4
Hawaii	Region 9
Idaho	Region 10
Illinois	Region 5
Indiana	Region 5
Iowa	Region 7
Kansas	Region 7
Kentucky	Region 4
Louisiana	Region 6
Maine	Region 1
Maryland	Region 3
Massachusetts	Region 1
Michigan	Region 5
Minnesota	Region 5
Mississippi	Region 4
Missouri	Region 7
Montana	Region 8
Nebraska	Region 7
Nevada	Region 9
New Hampshire	Region 1
New Jersey	Region 2
New Mexico	Region 6
New York	Region 2
North Carolina	Region 4
North Dakota	Region 8

REGION 1

Areas Served: Connecticut, Maine, Massachusetts, New Hampshire, Rhode Island, Vermont

Regional Office:
Small Business Administration
60 Batterymarch, 10th floor
Boston, MA 02210
(617) 451-2030

District Offices:

10 Causeway Street, 10th Floor
Boston, MA 02214
(617) 565-5590

Federal Building
40 Western Ave., Room 512
Augusta, ME 04330
(207) 622-8378

55 Pleasant Street, Room 210
Concord, NH 03301
(603) 225-1400

Federal Building
330 Main Street, 2nd Floor
Hartford, CT 06106
(203) 240-4700

Federal Building
87 State Street, Room 205
Montpelier, VT 05602
(802) 828-4474

380 Westminster Mall
Providence, RI 02903
(401) 528-4586

REGION 2

Areas Served: New Jersey, New York, Puerto Rico, Virgin Islands

Regional Office:
Small Business Administration
26 Federal Plaza, Room 3100
New York, NY 10278
(212) 264-7772

District Offices:

Carlos Chardon Avenue, Rm 691
Hato Rey, PR 00918
(809) 753-4002

4 C&D State Sion Farm, Room 7
Christiansted, St. Croix, VI 00820

Federal Office Building
Veterans Drive, Room 210
St. Thomas, VI 00801
(809) 77-48530

60 Park Place, 4th Floor
Newark, NJ 07102
(201) 645-2434

26 Federal Plaza, Room 3100
New York, NY 10278
(212) 264-4355

100 S. Clinton St., Rm 1071
Syracuse, NY 13260
(315) 423-5383

REGION 3

Areas Served: Delaware, District of Columbia, Maryland, Pennsylvania, Virginia, West Virginia

Regional Office:
Small Business Administration
475 Allendale Road, Suite 201
King of Prussia, PA 19406
(215) 962-3800

District Offices:

168 W. Main St., 5th Floor
Clarksburg, WV 26301
(304) 623-5631

960 Penn Avenue, 5th Floor
Pittsburgh, PA 15222
(412) 644-2780

Federal Building
400 N. 8th St., Room 3015
Richmond, VA 23240
(804) 771-2617

1111 18th Street, NW, 6th Floor
Washington, DC 20036
(202) 634-4950

Equitable Building, 3rd Floor
10 N. Calvert Street
Baltimore, MD 21202
(301) 962-4392

REGION 4

Areas Served: Alabama, Florida,
Georgia, Kentucky, Mississippi, North
Carolina, South Carolina, Tennessee

Regional Office:
Small Business Administration
1375 Peachtree St, NE, 5th Floor
Atlanta, GA 30367
(404) 347-2797

District Offices:

2121 8th Ave. N., Suite 200
Birmingham, AL 35203
(205) 731-1344

1720 Peachtree Rd., NW, 6th Floor
Atlanta, GA 30309
(404) 347-2441

222 South Church St., Room 300
Charlotte, NC 28201
(704) 371-6563

1835 Assembly Street, Room 358
Columbia, SC 29201
(803) 765-5376

100 W. Capitol St., Room 322
Jackson, MS 39269
(601) 965-4378

Federal Building
400 W. Bay St., Room 261
Jacksonville, FL 32202
(904) 791-3782

Federal Building
600 Federal Place, Room 188
Louisville, KY 40202
(502) 582-5976

1320 S. Dixie Highway, Ste 501
Coral Gables, Fl 33136
(305) 536-5521

404 James Robertson Pkwy, Rm 1012
Nashville, TN 37219
(615) 736-5887

REGION 5

Areas Served: Illinois, Indiana,
Michigan, Minnesota, Ohio, Wisconsi

Regional Office:
Small Business Administration
Federal Building
230 S. Dearborn Street, Rm 510
Chicago, IL 60604
(312) 353-0359

District Offices:

219 South Dearborn St., Rm 437
Chicago, IL 60604
(312) 353-4528

1240 E. 9th Street, Room 317
Cleveland, OH 44199
(216) 522-4180

85 Marconi Blvd., Room 512
Columbus, OH 43215
(614) 469-6860

477 Michigan Avenue, Room 515
Detroit, MI 48226
(313) 226-6075

575 N. Pennsylvania St., Rm 578
Indianapolis, IN 46204
(317) 269-7272

212 E. Washington Ave., Rm 213
Madison, WI 53707
(608) 264-5205

100 N. 5th St., Suite 610-C
Minneapolis, MN 55403
(612) 370-2324

REGION 6

Areas Served: Arkansas, Louisiana, New Mexico, Oklahoma, Texas

Regional Office:
Small Business Administration
8625 King George Dr., Bldg. C
Dallas, TX 75235
(214) 767-7643

District Offices:

5000 Marble Ave., NE, Rm 320
Albuquerque, NM 87110
(505) 262-6171

2525 Murworth, Room 112
Houston, TX 77054
(713) 660-4401

P.O. and Courthouse Bldg.
320 W. Capitol Ave., Rm 601
Little Rock, AR 72201
(501) 378-5871

1611 Tenth Avenue, Suite 200
Lubbock, TX 79401
(806) 762-7462

222 East Van Buren St., Rm 500
Harlingen, TX 78550
(512) 427-8533

1661 Canal Street, Suite 2000
New Orleans, LA 70112
(504) 589-6685

200 NW 5th Street, Room 670
Oklahoma City, OK 73102
(405) 231-4405

7400 Blanco Road, Suite 200
San Antonio, TX 78206
(512) 229-4535

1100 Commerce St., Room 3C36
Dallas, TX 79935
(214) 767-0605

REGION 7

Areas Served: Iowa, Kansas, Missouri, Nebraska

Regional Office:
911 Walnut Street, 13th Floor
Kansas City, MO 64106
(816) 374-5288

District Offices:

New Federal Building
210 Walnut Street, Room 749
Des Moines, IA 50309
(515) 284-4422

373 Collins Road NE, Room 100
Cedar Rapids, IA 52402
(319) 399-2571

1145 Mill Valley Road
Omaha, NE 68154
(402) 221-4691

815 Olive Street, Room 242
St. Louis, MO 63101
(314) 425-6600

1103 Grand Avenue, 6th Floor
Kansas City, MO 64106
(816) 374-3419

110 East Waterman St., 1st Fl
Wichita, KS 67202
(316) 269-6571

REGION 8

Areas Served: Colorado, Montana, North Dakota, South Dakota, Utah, Wyoming

Regional Office:
Small Business Administration
999 18th Street, Suite 701
Denver, CO 80202
(303) 294-7001

District Offices:

Federal Building
100 East B Street, Room 4001
Casper, WY 82602
(307) 261-5761

Federal Building
657 2nd Ave. North, Room 218
Fargo, ND 58108
(701) 237-5771 Ext. 5131

301 South Park Ave., Room 528
Helena, MT 59626
(406) 449-5381

Federal Building
125 South State St., Room 2237
Salt Lake City, UT 84138
(801) 524-5800

101 S. Main Ave., Suite 101
Sioux Falls, SD 57102
(605) 336-2980 Ext. 231

721 19th Street, Room 407
Denver, CO 80202
(303) 844-2607

REGION 9

Areas Served: Arizona, California,
Hawaii, Nevada, Pacific Islands

Regional Office:
Small Buisness Administration
Federal Building
450 Golden Gate Avenue
San Francisco, CA 94102
(415) 556-7487

District Offices:

300 Ala Moana, Room 2213
Honolulu, HI 96850
(808) 541-2990

350 S. Figueroa St., 6th Floor
Los Angeles, CA 90071
(213) 894-2956

2202 Monterey St., Suite 108
Fresno, CA 93721
(209) 487-5189

211 Main Street, 4th Floor
San Francisco, CA 94105
(415) 974-0642

2005 N. Central Ave., 5th Floor
Phoenix, AZ 85004
(602) 261-3732

880 Front Street, Room 4-S-29
San Diego, CA 92188
(619) 557-5440

301 E. Stewart St., Room 301
Las Vegas, NV 89125
(702) 388-6611

REGION 10

Areas Served: Alaska, Idaho, Oregon,
Washington

Regional Office:
Small Business Administration
2615 4th Avenue, Room 440
Seattle, WA 98121
(206) 442-5676

District Offices:

8th & C Streets
Anchorage, AK 99513
(907) 271-4022

1020 Main Street, Suite 290
Boise, ID 83702
(208) 334-1696

1220 SW Third Ave., Room 676
Portland, OR 97204
(503) 221-2682

W. 920 Riverside Ave., Rm 651
Spokane, WA 99210
(509) 456-3783

915 Second Ave., Room 1792
Seattle, WA 98174
(206) 442-5534

109

NOTES

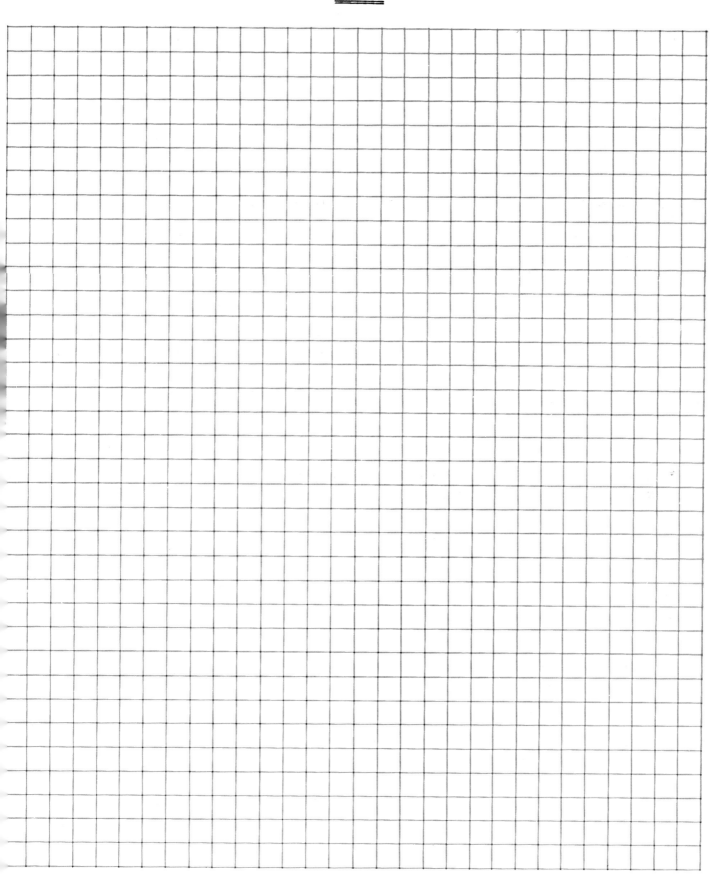

NOTES

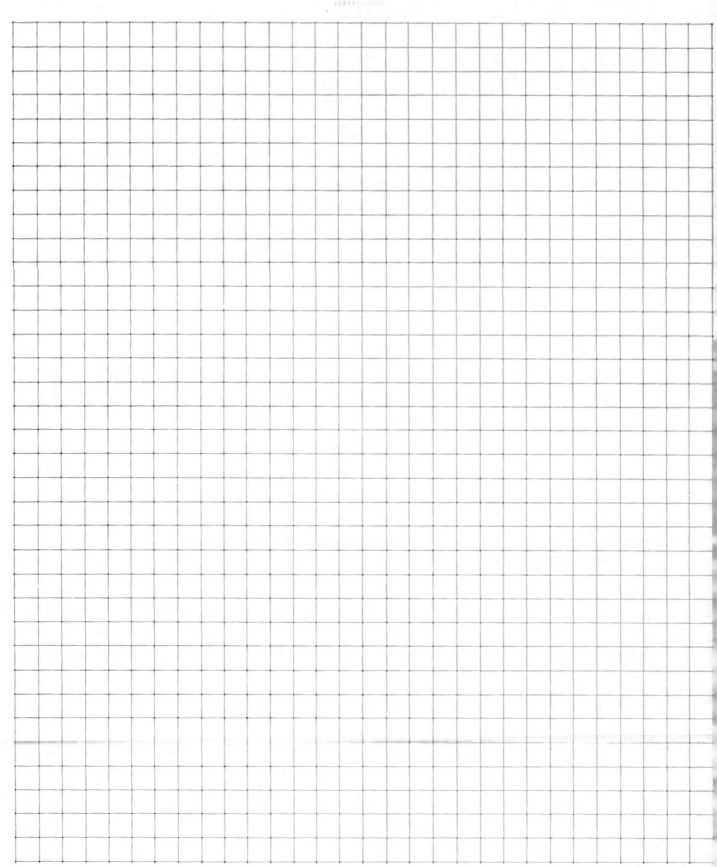

NOTES

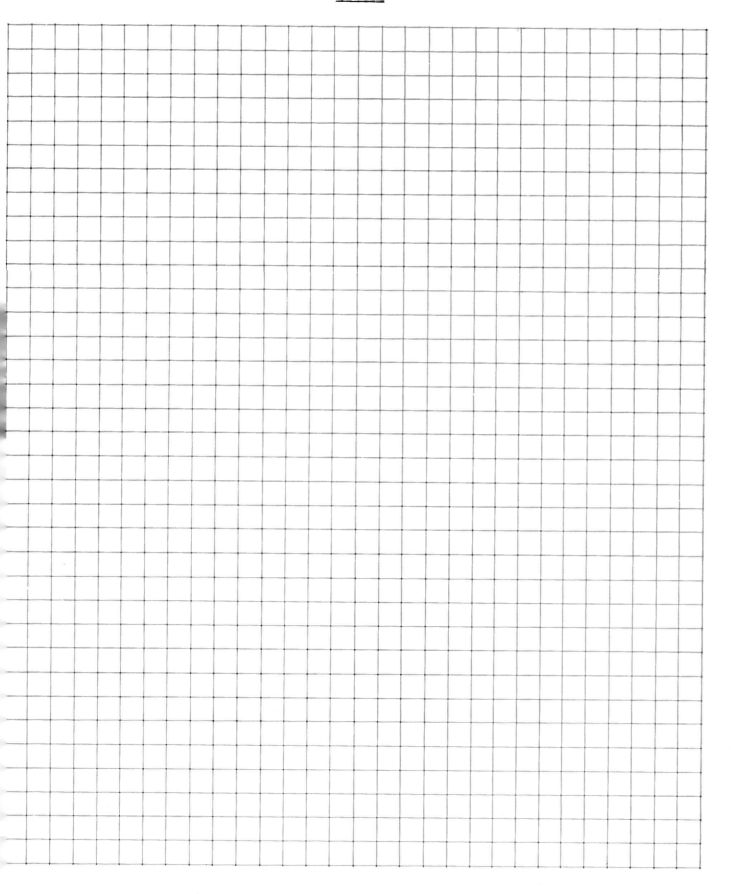

NOTES